THE ELEMENTS OF STYLE

WILLIAM STRUNK, JR.

HOW TO
SPEAK AND WRITE
CORRECTLY

JOSEPH DEVLIN, M.A.

Originally published by

ITHACA, N.Y.: W.P. HUMPHREY

www.bnpublishing.com

Printed in the U.S.A.

The Elements of Style
William Strunk, Jr.

Asserting that one must first know the rules to break them, this classic reference book is a must-have for any student and conscientious writer. Intended for use in which the practice of composition is combined with the study of literature, it gives in brief space the principal requirements of plain English style and concentrates attention on the rules of usage and principles of composition most commonly violated.

I. INTRODUCTORY

This book is intended for use in English courses in which the practice of composition is combined with the study of literature. It aims to give in brief space the principal requirements of plain English style. It aims to lighten the task of instructor and student by concentrating attention (in Chapters II and III) on a few essentials, the rules of usage and principles of composition most commonly violated. The numbers of the sections may be used as references in correcting manuscript.

The book covers only a small portion of the field of English style, but the experience of its writer has been that once past the essentials, students profit most by individual instruction based on the problems of their own work, and that each instructor has his own body of theory, which he prefers to that offered by any textbook.

The writer's colleagues in the Department of English in Cornell University have greatly helped him in the preparation of his manuscript. Mr. George M 19f cLane Wood has kindly consented to the inclusion under Rule 11 of some material from his *Suggestions to Authors.*

The following books are recommended for reference or further study: in connection with Chapters II and IV, F. Howard Collins, *Author and Printer* (Henry Frowde); Chicago University Press, *Manual of Style;* T. L. De Vinne *Cor f52 rect Composition* (The Century Company); Horace Hart, *Rules for Compositors and Printers* (Oxford University Press); George McLane Wood, *Extracts from the Style-Book of the Government Printing Office* (United States Geological Survey); in connection with Chapters III and V, Sir Arthur Quiller-Couch, *The Art of Writing* (Putnams), especially the chapter, Interlude on Jargon; George McLane Wood, *Suggestions to Authors* (United States Geological Survey); John Leslie Hall, *English Usage* (Scott, Foresman and Co.); James P. Kelly, *Workmanship in Words* (Little, Brown and Co.).

It is an old observation that the best writers sometimes disregard the rules of rhetoric. When they do so, however, the reader will usually find in the sentence some compensating merit, attained at the cost of the violation. Unless he is certain of doing as well, he will probably do best to follow the rules. After he has learned, by their guidance, to write plain English adequate for everyday uses, let him look, for the secrets of style, to the study of the masters of literature.

II. ELEMENTARY RULES OF USAGE

1.   **Form the possessive singular of nouns with 's.**

Follow this rule whatever the final consonant. Thus write,

Charles's friend
Burns's poems
the witch's malice

This is the usage of the United States Government Printing Office and of the Oxford University Press.

Exceptions are the possessives of ancient proper names in *-es* and *-is*, such forms as *for conscience' sake, for righteousness' sake*. But such forms as *Achilles' heel, Moses' laws, Isis' temple* are commonly replaced by

the heel of Achilles
the laws of Moses
the temple of Isis

The pronominal possessives *hers, its, theirs, yours,* and *oneself* have no apostrophe.

2.   **In a series of three or more terms with a single conjunction, use a comma after each term except the last.**

Thus write,

> red, white, and blue

> honest, energetic, but headstrong

> He opened the letter, read it, and made a note of its contents.

This is also the usage of the Government Printing Office and of the Oxford University Press.

In the names of business firms the last comma is omitted, as

> Brown, Shipley and Company

The abbreviation etc., even if only a single term comes before it, is always preceded by a comma.

3.　　**Enclose parenthetic expressions between commas.**

> The best way to see a country, unless you are pressed for time, is to travel on foot.

This rule is difficult to apply; it is frequently hard to decide whether a single word, such as however, or a brief phrase, is or is not parenthetic. If the interruption to the flow of the sentence is but slight, the writer may safely omit the commas. But whether the interruption be slight or considerable, he must never omit one comma and leave the other. Such punctuation as

> Marjorie's husband, Colonel Nelson paid us a visit yesterday,

or

> My brother you will be pleased to hear, is now in perfect health,

is indefensible.

8

Non-restrictive relative clauses are, in accordance with this rule, set off by commas.

> The audience, which had at first been indifferent, became more and more interested.

Similar clauses introduced by *where* and *when* are similarly punctuated.

> In 1769, when Napoleon was born, Corsica had but recently been acquired by France.

> Nether Stowey, where Coleridge wrote *The Rime of the Ancient Mariner*, is a few miles from Bridgewater.

In these sentences the clauses introduced by *which, when,* and *where* are non-restrictive; they do not limit the application of the words on which they depend, but add, parenthetically, statements supplementing those in the principal clauses. Each sentence is a combination of two statments which might have been made independently.

> The audience was at first indifferent. Later it became more and more interested.

> Napoleon was born in 1769. At that time Corsica had but recently been acquired by France.

> Coleridge wrote *The Rime of the Ancient Mariner* at Nether Stowey. Nether Stowey is only a few miles from Bridgewater.

Restrictive relative clauses are not set off by commas.

> The candidate who best meets these requirements will obtain the place.

In this sentence the relative clause restricts the application of the word *candidate* to a single person. Unlike those above, the sentence cannot be split into two independent statements.

The abbreviations etc. and *jr.* are always preceded by a comma, and except at the end of a sentence, followed by one.

Similar in principle to the enclosing of parenthetic expressions between commas is the setting off by commas of phrases or dependent clauses preceding or following the main clause of a sentence. The sentences quoted in this section and under Rules 4, 5, 6, 7, 16, and 18 should afford sufficient guidance.

If a parenthetic expression is preceded by a conjunction, place the first comma before the conjunction, not after it.

> He saw us coming, and unaware that we had learned of his treachery, greeted us with a smile.

4. **Place a comma before *and* or *but* introducing an independent clause.**

> The early records of the city have disappeared, and the story of its first years can no longer be reconstructed.

> The situation is perilous, but there is still one chance of escape.

Sentences of this type, isolated from their context, may seem to be in need of rewriting. As they make complete sense when the comma is reached, the second clause has the appearance of an afterthought. Further, *and,* is the least specific of connectives. Used between independent clauses, it indicates only that a relation exists between them without defining that relation. In the example above, the relation is that of cause and result. The two sentences might be rewritten:

> As the early records of the city have disappeared, the story of its first years can no longer be reconstructed.

> Although the situation is perilous, there is still one chance of escape.

Or the subordinate clauses might be replaced by phrases:

> Owing to the disappearance of the early records of the city, the story of its first years can no longer be reconstructed.

> In this perilous situation, there is still one chance of escape.

But a writer may err by making his sentences too uniformly compact and periodic, and an occasional loose sentence prevents the style from becoming too formal and gives the reader a certain relief. Consequently, loose sentences of the type first quoted are common in easy, unstudied writing. But a writer should be careful not to construct too many of his sentences after this pattern (see Rule 14*).

Two-part sentences of which the second member is introduced by *as* (in the sense of *because*), *for, or, nor,* and *while* (in the sense of *and at the same time*) likewise require a comma before the conjunction.

If a dependent clause, or an introductory phrase requiring to be set off by a comma, precedes the second independent clause, no comma is needed after the conjunction.

> The situation is perilous, but if we are prepared to act promptly, there is still one chance of escape.

For two-part sentences connected by an adverb, see the next section.

5.   **Do not join independent clauses by a comma.**

If two or more clauses, grammatically complete and not joined by a conjunction, are to form a single compound sentence, the proper mark of punctuation is a semicolon.

> Stevenson's romances are entertaining; they are full of exciting adventures.

> It is nearly half past five; we cannot reach town before dark.

It is of course equally correct to write the above as two sentences each, replacing the semicolons by periods.

---

* Avoid a succession of loose sentences.

> Stevenson's romances are entertaining. They are full of exciting adventures.

> It is nearly half past five. We cannot reach town before dark.

If a conjunction is inserted, the proper mark is a comma (Rule 4*).

> Stevenson's romances are entertaining, for they are full of exciting adventures.

> It is nearly half past five, and we cannot reach town before dark.

Note that if the second clause is preceded by an adverb, such as *accordingly, besides, so, then, therefore,* or *thus,* and not by a conjunction, the semicolon is still required.

> I had never been in the place before; so I had difficulty in finding my way about.

In general, however, it is best, in writing, to avoid using *so* in this manner; there is danger that the writer who uses it at all may use it too often. A simple correction, usually serviceable, is to omit the word *so,* and begin the first clause with *as:*

> As I had never been in the place before, I had difficulty in finding my way about.

If the clauses are very short, and are alike in form, a comma is usually permissible:

> Man proposes, God disposes.

> The gate swung apart, the bridge fell, the portcullis was drawn up.

---

* Place a comma before *and* or *but* introducing an independent clause.

6.   **Do not break sentences in two.**

In other words, do not use periods for commas.

> I met them on a Cunard liner several years ago. Coming home from Liverpool to New York.

> He was an interesting talker. A man who had traveled all over the world, and lived in half a dozen countries.

In both these examples, the first period should be replaced by a comma, and the following word begun with a small letter.

It is permissible to make an emphatic word or expression serve the purpose of a sentence and to punctuate it accordingly:

> Again and again he called out. No reply.

The writer must, however, be certain that the emphasis is warranted, and that he will not be suspected of a mere blunder in punctuation.

Rules 3,4,5 and 6 cover the most important principles in the punctuation of ordinary sentences; they should be so thoroughly mastered that their application becomes second nature.

7.   **A participial phrase at the beginning of a sentence must refer to the grammatical subject.**

> Walking slowly down the road, he saw a woman accompanied by two children.

13

The word *walking* refers to the subject of the sentence, not to the woman. If the writer wishes to make it refer to the woman, he must recast the sentence:

> He saw a woman, accompanied by two children, walking slowly down the road.

Participial phrases preceded by a conjunction or by a preposition, nouns in apposition, adjectives, and adjective phrases come under the same rule if they begin the sentence.

On arriving in Chicago, his friends met him at the station.	When he arrived (or, On his arrival) in Chicago, his friends met him at the station.
A soldier of proved valor, they entrusted him with the defence of the city.	A soldier of proved valor, he was entrusted with the defence of the city.
Young and inexperienced, the task seemed easy to me.	Young and inexperienced, I thought the task easy.
Without a friend to counsel him, the temptation proved irresistible.	Without a friend to counsel him, he found the temptation irresistible.

Sentences violating this rule are often ludicrous.

> Being in a dilapidated condition, I was able to buy the house very cheap.

8.   **Divide words at line-ends, in accordance with their formation and pronunciation.**

If there is room at the end of a line for one or more syllables of a word, but not for the whole word, divide the word, unless this involves cutting off only a single letter, or cutting off only two letters of a long word. No hard and fast rule for all words can be laid down. The principles most frequently applicable are:

A.   Divide the word according to its formation:

> know-ledge (not knowl-edge); Shake-speare (not Shakes-peare); de-scribe (not des-cribe); atmo-sphere (not atmos-phere);

B.   Divide "on the vowel:"

> edi-ble (not ed-ible); propo-sition; ordi-nary; espe-cial; reli-gious; oppo-nents; regu-lar; classi-fi-ca-tion (three divisions possible); deco-rative; presi-dent;

C.   Divide between double letters, unless they come at the end of the simple form of the word:

> Apen-nines; Cincin-nati; refer-ring; but tell-ing.

The treatment of consonants in combination is best shown from examples:

> for-tune; pic-ture; presump-tuous; illus-tration; sub-stan-tial (either division); indus-try; instruc-tion; sug-ges-tion; incen-diary.

The student will do well to examine the syllable-division in a number of pages of any carefully printed book.

III. ELEMENTARY PRINCIPLES OF COMPOSITION

9.   **Make the paragraph the unit of composition: one paragraph to each topic.**

If the subject on which you are writing is of slight extent, or if you intend to treat it very briefly, there may be no need of subdividing it into topics. Thus a brief description, a brief summary of a literary work, a brief account of a single incident, a narrative merely outlining an action, the setting forth of a single idea, any one of these is best written in a single paragraph. After the paragraph has been written, it should be examined to see whether subdivision will not improve it.

Ordinarily, however, a subject requires subdivision into topics, each of which should be made the subject of a paragraph. The object of treating each topic in a paragraph by itself is, of course, to aid the reader. The beginning of each paragraph is a signal to him that a new step in the development of the subject has been reached.

The extent of subdivision will vary with the length of the composition. For example, a short notice of a book or poem might consist of a single paragraph. One slightly longer might consist of two paragraphs:

    A.   Account of the work.
    B.   Critical discussion.

A report on a poem, written for a class in literature, might consist of seven paragraphs:

    C.   Facts of composition and publication.
    D.   Kind of poem; metrical form.
    E.   Subject.
    F.   Treatment of subject.
    G.   For what chiefly remarkable.
    H.   Wherein characteristic of the writer.
    I.   Relationship to other works.

The contents of paragraphs C and D would vary with the poem. Usually, paragraph C would indicate the actual or imagined circumstances of the poem (the situation), if these call for explanation, and would then state the subject and outline its development. If the poem is a narrative in the third person throughout, paragraph C need contain no more than a concise summary of the action. Paragraph D would indicate the leading ideas and show how they are made prominent, or would indicate what points in the narrative are chiefly emphasized.

A novel might be discussed under the heads:

      J.   Setting.
      K.   Plot.
      L.   Characters.
      M.   Purpose.

A historical event might be discussed under the heads:

      N.   What led up to the event.
      O.   Account of the event.
      P.   What the event led up to.

In treating either of these last two subjects, the writer would probably find it necessary to subdivide one or more of the topics here given.

As a rule, single sentences should not be written or printed as paragraphs. An exception may be made of sentences of transition, indicating the relation between the parts of an exposition or argument.

In dialogue, each speech, even if only a single word, is a paragraph by itself; that is, a new paragraph begins with each change of speaker. The application of this rule, when dialogue and narrative are combined, is best learned from examples in well-printed works of fiction.

10.   **As a rule, begin each paragraph with a topic sentence; end it in conformity with the beginning.**

Again, the object is to aid the reader. The practice here recommended enables him to discover the purpose of each paragraph as he begins to read it, and to retain the purpose in mind as he ends it. For this reason, the most generally useful kind of paragraph, particularly in exposition and argument, is that in which

      A.   the topic sentence comes at or near the beginning;
      B.   the succeeding sentences explain or establish or develop the statement made in the topic sentence; and
      C.   the final sentence either emphasizes the thought of the topic sentence or states some important consequence.

Ending with a digression, or with an unimportant detail, is particularly to be avoided.

If the paragraph forms part of a larger composition, its relation to what precedes, or its function as a part of the whole, may need to be expressed. This can sometimes be done by a mere word or phrase (*again; therefore; for the same reason*) in the topic sentence. Sometimes, however, it is expedient to precede the topic sentence by one or more sentences of introduction or transition. If more than one such sentence is required, it is generally better to set apart the transitional sentences as a separate paragraph.

According to the writer's purpose, he may, as indicated above, relate the body of the paragraph to the topic sentence in one or more of several different ways. He may make the meaning of the topic sentence clearer by restating it in other forms, by defining its terms, by denying the converse, by giving illustrations or specific instances; he may establish it by proofs; or he may develop it by showing its implications and consequences. In a long paragraph, he may carry out several of these processes.

1 Now, to be properly enjoyed, a walking tour should be gone upon alone.	**1** Topic sentence.
2 If you go in a company, or even in pairs, it is no longer a walking tour in anything but name; it is something else and more in the nature of a picnic.	**2** The meaning made clearer by denial of the contrary.
3 A walking tour should be gone upon alone, because freedom is of the essence; because you should be able to stop and go on, and follow this way or that, as the freak takes you; and because you must have your own pace, and neither trot alongside a champion walker, nor mince in time with a girl.	**3** The topic sentence repeated, in abridged form, and supported by three reasons; the meaning of the third ("you must have your own pace") made clearer by denying the converse.
4 And you must be open to all impressions and let your thoughts take colour from what you see.	**4** A fourth reason, stated in two forms.
5 You should be as a pipe for any wind to play upon.	**5** The same reason, stated in still another form.
6 "I cannot see the wit," says Hazlitt, "of walking and talking at the same time.	**6-7** The same reason as stated by Hazlitt.
7 When I am in the country, I wish to vegetate like the country," which is the gist of all that can be said upon the matter.	
8 There should be no cackle of voices at your elbow, to jar on the meditative silence of the morning.	**8** Repetition, in paraphrase, of the quotation from Hazlitt.
9 And so long as a man is reasoning he cannot surrender himself to that fine intoxication that comes of much motion in the open air, that begins in a sort of dazzle and sluggishness of the brain, and ends in a peace that passes comprehension.—Stevenson, *Walking Tours*.	**9** Final statement of the fourth reason, in language amplified and heightened to form a strong conclusion.

1 It was chiefly in the eighteenth century that a very different conception of history grew up.	**1** Topic sentence.
2 Historians then came to believe that their task was not so much to paint a picture as to solve a problem; to explain or illustrate the successive phases of national growth, prosperity, and adversity.	**2** The meaning of the topic sentence made clearer; the new conception of history defined.
3 The history of morals, of industry, of intellect, and of art; the changes that take place in manners or beliefs; the dominant ideas that prevailed in successive periods; the rise, fall, and modification of political constitutions; in a word, all the conditions of national well-being became the subjects of their works.	**3** The definition expanded.
4 They sought rather to write a history of peoples than a history of kings.	**4** The definition explained by contrast.
5 They looked especially in history for the chain of causes and effects.	**5** The definition supplemented: another element in the new conception of history.
6 They undertook to study in the past the physiology of nations, and hoped by applying the experimental method on a large scale to deduce some lessons of real value about the conditions on which the welfare of society mainly depend.— Lecky, *The Political Value of History.*	**6** Conclusion: an important consequence of the new conception of history.

In narration and description the paragraph sometimes begins with a concise, comprehensive statement serving to hold together the details that follow.

The breeze served us admirably.
The campaign opened with a series of reverses.
The next ten or twelve pages were filled with a curious set of entries.

But this device, if too often used, would become a mannerism. More commonly the opening sentence simply indicates by its subject with what the paragraph is to be principally concerned.

> At length I thought I might return towards the stockade.
>
> He picked up the heavy lamp from the table and began to explore.
>
> Another flight of steps, and they emerged on the roof.

The brief paragraphs of animated narrative, however, are often without even this semblance of a topic sentence. The break between them serves the purpose of a rhetorical pause, throwing into prominence some detail of the action.

11.   **Use the active voice.**

The active voice is usually more direct and vigorous than the passive:

> I shall always remember my first visit to Boston.

This is much better than

> My first visit to Boston will always be remembered by me.

The latter sentence is less direct, less bold, and less concise. If the writer tries to make it more concise by omitting "by me,"

> My first visit to Boston will always be remembered,

it becomes indefinite: is it the writer, or some person undisclosed, or the world at large, that will always remember this visit?

This rule does not, of course, mean that the writer should entirely discard the passive voice, which is frequently convenient and sometimes necessary.

The dramatists of the Restoration are little esteemed to-day.	
Modern readers have little esteem for the dramatists of the Restoration.	

The first would be the right form in a paragraph on the dramatists of the Restoration; the second, in a paragraph on the tastes of modern readers. The need of making a particular word the subject of the sentence will often, as in these examples, determine which voice is to be used.

The habitual use of the active voice, however, makes for forcible writing. This is true not only in narrative principally concerned with action, but in writing of any kind. Many a tame sentence of description or exposition can be made lively and emphatic by substituting a transitive in the active voice for some such perfunctory expression as *there is,* or *could be heard.*

There were a great number of dead leaves lying on the ground.	Dead leaves covered the ground.
The sound of the falls could still be heard.	The sound of the falls still reached our ears.
The reason that he left college was that his health became impaired.	Failing health compelled him to leave college.
It was not long before he was very sorry that he had said what he had.	He soon repented his words.

As a rule, avoid making one passive depend directly upon another.

Gold was not allowed to be exported.	It was forbidden to export gold (The export of gold was prohibited).
He has been proved to have been seen entering the building.	It has been proved that he was seen to enter the building.

In both the examples above, before correction, the word properly related to the second passive is made the subject of the first.

A common fault is to use as the subject of a passive construction a noun which expresses the entire action, leaving to the verb no function beyond that of completing the sentence.

A survey of this region was made in 1900.	This region was surveyed in 1900.
Mobilization of the army was rapidly carried out.	The army was rapidly mobilized.
Confirmation of these reports cannot be obtained.	These reports cannot be confirmed.

Compare the sentence, "The export of gold was prohibited," in which the predicate "was prohibited" expresses something not implied in "export."

12. **Put statements in positive form.**

Make definite assertions. Avoid tame, colorless, hesitating, non-committal language. Use the word *not* as a means of denial or in antithesis, never as a means of evasion.

He was not very often on time.	He usually came late.
He did not think that studying Latin was much use.	He thought the study of Latin useless.
The Taming of the Shrew is rather weak in spots. Shakespeare does not portray Katharine as a very admirable character, nor does Bianca remain long in memory as an important character in Shakespeare's works.	The women in *The Taming of the Shrew* are unattractive. Katharine is disagreeable, Bianca insignificant.

The last example, before correction, is indefinite as well as negative. The corrected version, consequently, is simply a guess at the writer's intention.

All three examples show the weakness inherent in the word *not*. Consciously or unconsciously, the reader is dissatisfied with being told only what is not; he wishes to be told what is. Hence, as a rule, it is better to express a negative in positive form.

not honest	dishonest
not important	trifling
did not remember	forgot
did not pay any attention to	ignored
did not have much confidence in	distrusted

The antithesis of negative and positive is strong:

Not charity, but simple justice.
Not that I loved Caesar less, but Rome the more.

Negative words other than *not* are usually strong:

The sun never sets upon the British flag.

13.   **Omit needless words.**

Vigorous writing is concise. A sentence should contain no unnecessary words, a paragraph no unnecessary sentences, for the same reason that a drawing should have no unnecessary lines and a machine no unnecessary parts. This requires not that the writer make all his sentences short, or that he avoid all detail and treat his subjects only in outline, but that every word tell.

Many expressions in common use violate this principle:

the question as to whether	whether (the question whether)
there is no doubt but that	no doubt (doubtless)
used for fuel purposes	used for fuel
he is a man who	he
in a hasty manner	hastily
this is a subject which	this subject
His story is a strange one.	His story is strange.

In especial the expression *the fact that* should be revised out of every sentence in which it occurs.

owing to the fact that	since (because)
in spite of the fact that	though (although)
call your attention to the fact that	remind you (notify you)
I was unaware of the fact that	I was unaware that (did not know)
the fact that he had not succeeded	his failure
the fact that I had arrived	my arrival

See also under case, *character, nature, system* in Chapter V.

Who is, which was, and the like are often superfluous.

25

His brother, who is a member of the same firm	His brother, a member of the same firm
Trafalgar, which was Nelson's last battle	Trafalgar, Nelson's last battle

As positive statement is more concise than negative, and the active voice more concise than the passive, many of the examples given under Rules 11 and 12 illustrate this rule as well.

A common violation of conciseness is the presentation of a single complex idea, step by step, in a series of sentences which might to advantage be combined into one.

Macbeth was very ambitious. This led him to wish to become king of Scotland. The witches told him that this wish of his would come true. The king of Scotland at this time was Duncan. Encouraged by his wife, Macbeth murdered Duncan. He was thus enabled to succeed Duncan as king. (55 words.)	Encouraged by his wife, Macbeth achieved his ambition and realized the prediction of the witches by murdering Duncan and becoming king of Scotland in his place. (26 words.)

14. **Avoid a succession of loose sentences.**

This rule refers especially to loose sentences of a particular type, those consisting of two co-ordinate clauses, the second introduced by a conjunction or relative. Although single sentences of this type may be unexceptionable[*], a series soon becomes monotonous and tedious.

An unskilful writer will sometimes construct a whole paragraph of sentences of this kind, using as connectives *and, but,* and less frequently, *who, which, when, where,* and *while,* these last in non-restrictive senses[**].

The third concert of the subscription series was given last evening, and a large audience was in attendance. Mr. Edward Appleton was the soloist, and the Boston Symphony Orchestra furnished the instrumental music. The former showed himself to be an artist of the first rank, while the latter proved itself fully deserving of its high reputation. The interest aroused by the series has been very gratifying to the Committee, and it is planned to give a similar series annually hereafter. The fourth concert will be given on Tuesday, May 10, when an equally attractive programme will be presented.

---

[*] Place a comma before *and* or *but* introducing an independent clause.
[**] Enclose parenthetic expressions between commas.

Apart from its triteness and emptiness, the paragraph above is bad because of the structure of its sentences, with their mechanical symmetry and sing-song. Contrast with them the sentences in the paragraphs quoted under Rule 10, or in any piece of good English prose, as the preface (Before the Curtain) to *Vanity Fair*.

If the writer finds that he has written a series of sentences of the type described, he should recast enough of them to remove the monotony, replacing them by simple sentences, by sentences of two clauses joined by a semicolon, by periodic sentences of two clauses, by sentences, loose or periodic, of three clauses—whichever best represent the real relations of the thought.

15. **Express co-ordinate ideas in similar form.**

This principle, that of parallel construction, requires that expressions of similar content and function should be outwardly similar. The likeness of form enables the reader to recognize more readily the likeness of content and function. Familiar instances from the Bible are the Ten Commandments, the Beatitudes, and the petitions of the Lord's Prayer.

The unskilful writer often violates this principle, from a mistaken belief that he should constantly vary the form of his expressions. It is true that in repeating a statement in order to emphasize it he may have need to vary its form. For illustration, see the paragraph from Stevenson quoted under Rule 10. But apart from this, he should follow the principle of parallel construction.

Formerly, science was taught by the textbook method, while now the laboratory method is employed.	Formerly, science was taught by the textbook method; now it is taught by the laboratory method.

The left-hand version gives the impression that the writer is undecided or timid; he seems unable or afraid to choose one form of expression and hold to it. The right-hand version shows that the writer has at least made his choice and abided by it.

By this principle, an article or a preposition applying to all the members of a series must either be used only before the first term or else be repeated before each term.

The French, the Italians, Spanish, and Portuguese	The French, the Italians, the Spanish, and the Portuguese
In spring, summer, or in winter	In spring, summer, or winter (In spring, in summer, or in winter)

Correlative expressions (*both, and; not, but; not only, but also; either, or; first, second, third;* and the like) should be followed by the same grammatical construction. Many violations of this rule can be corrected by rearranging the sentence.

It was both a long ceremony and very tedious.	The ceremony was both long and tedious.
A time not for words, but action	A time not for words, but for action
Either you must grant his request or incur his ill will.	You must either grant his request or incur his ill will.
My objections are, first, the injustice of the measure; second, that it is unconstitutional.	My objections are, first, that the measure is unjust; second, that it is unconstitutional.

See also the third example under Rule 12 and the last under Rule 13.

It may be asked, what if a writer needs to express a very large number of similar ideas, say twenty? Must he write twenty consecutive sentences of the same pattern? On closer examination he will probably find that the difficulty is imaginary, that his twenty ideas can be classified in groups, and that he need apply the principle only within each group. Otherwise he had best avoid the difficulty by putting his statements in the form of a table.

16. **Keep related words together.**

The position of the words in a sentence is the principal means of showing their relationship. The writer must therefore, so far as possible, bring together the words, and groups of words, that are related in thought, and keep apart those which are not so related.

The subject of a sentence and the principal verb should not, as a rule, be separated by a phrase or clause that can be transferred to the beginning.

Wordsworth, in the fifth book of *The Excursion,* gives a minute description.	In the fifth book of *The Excursion,* Wordsworth gives a minute description.
Cast iron, when treated in a Bessemer converter, is changed into	By treatment in a Bessemer converter, cast iron is changed into steel.

The objection is that the interposed phrase or clause needlessly interrupts the natural order of the main clause. This objection, however, does not usually hold when the order is interrupted only by a relative clause or by an expression in apposition. Nor does it hold in periodic sentences in which the interruption is a deliberately used means of creating suspense (see examples under Rule 18).

The relative pronoun should come, as a rule, immediately after its antecedent.

There was a look in his eye that boded mischief.	In his eye was a look that boded mischief.
He wrote three articles about his adventures in Spain, which were published in *Harper's Magazine.*	He published in *Harper's Magazine* three articles about his adventures in Spain.
This is a portrait of Benjamin Harrison, grandson of William Henry Harrison, who became President in 1889	This is a portrait of Benjamin Harrison, grandson of William Henry Harrison. He became President in 1889.

If the antecedent consists of a group of words, the relative comes at the end of the group, unless this would cause ambiguity.

The Superintendent of the Chicago Division, who	
A proposal to amend the Sherman Act, which has been variously judged	A proposal, which has been variously judged, to amend the Sherman Act
	A proposal to amend the much-debated Sherman Act
The grandson of William Henry Harrison, who	William Henry Harrison's grandson, Benjamin Harrison, who

A noun in apposition may come between antecedent and relative, because in such a combination no real ambiguity can arise.

The Duke of York, his brother, who was regarded with hostility by the Whigs

Modifiers should come, if possible next to the word they modify. If several expressions modify the same word, they should be so arranged that no wrong relation is suggested.

All the members were not present.	Not all the members were present.
He only found two mistakes.	He found only two mistakes.
Major R. E. Joyce will give a lecture on Tuesday evening in Bailey Hall, to which the public is invited, on "My Experiences in Mesopotamia" at eight P. M.	On Tuesday evening at eight P. M., Major R. E. Joyce will give in Bailey Hall a lecture on "My Experiences in Mesopotamia." The public is invited.

17.   **In summaries, keep to one tense.**

In summarizing the action of a drama, the writer should always use the present tense. In summarizing a poem, story, or novel, he should preferably use the present, though he may use the past if he prefers. If the summary is in the present tense, antecedent action should be expressed by the perfect; if in the past, by the past perfect.

> An unforeseen chance prevents Friar John from delivering Friar Lawrence's letter to Romeo. Juliet, meanwhile, owing to her father's arbitrary change of the day set for her wedding, has been compelled to drink the potion on Tuesday night, with the result that Balthasar informs Romeo of her supposed death before Friar Lawrence learns of the nondelivery of the letter.

But whichever tense be used in the summary, a past tense in indirect discourse or in indirect question remains unchanged.

> The Legate inquires who struck the blow.

Apart from the exceptions noted, whichever tense the writer chooses, he should use throughout. Shifting from one tense to the other gives the appearance of uncertainty and irresolution (compare Rule 15*).

In presenting the statements or the thought of some one else, as in summarizing an essay or reporting a speech, the writer should avoid intercalating such expressions as "he said," "he stated," "the speaker added," "the speaker then went on to say," "the author also thinks," or the like. He should indicate clearly at the outset, once for all, that what follows is summary, and then waste no words in repeating the notification.

In notebooks, in newspapers, in handbooks of literature, summaries of one kind or another may be indispensable, and for children in primary schools it is a useful exercise to retell a story in their own words. But in the criticism or interpretation of literature the writer should be careful to avoid dropping into summary. He may find it necessary to devote one or two sentences to indicating the subject, or the opening situation, of the work he is discussing; he may cite numerous details to illustrate its qualities. But he should aim to write an orderly discussion supported by evidence, not a summary with occasional comment. Similarly, if the scope of his discussion includes a number of works, he will as a rule do better not to take them up singly in chronological order, but to aim from the beginning at establishing general conclusions.

---

* Express co-ordinate ideas in similar form.

18.   **Place the emphatic words of a sentence at the end.**

The proper place for the word, or group of words, which the writer desires to make most prominent is usually the end of the sentence.

Humanity has hardly advanced in fortitude since that time, though it has advanced in many other ways.	Humanity, since that time, has advanced in many other ways, but it has hardly advanced in fortitude.
This steel is principally used for making razors, because of its hardness.	Because of its hardness, this steel is principally used in making razors.

The word or group of words entitled to this position of prominence is usually the logical predicate, that is, the *new* element in the sentence, as it is in the second example.

The effectiveness of the periodic sentence arises from the prominence which it gives to the main statement.

Four centuries ago, Christopher Columbus, one of the Italian mariners whom the decline of their own republics had put at the service of the world and of adventure, seeking for Spain a westward passage to the Indies as a set-off against the achievements of Portuguese discoverers, lighted on America.
With these hopes and in this belief I would urge you, laying aside all hindrance, thrusting away all private aims, to devote yourselves unswervingly and unflinchingly to the vigorous and successful prosecution of this war.

The other prominent position in the sentence is the beginning. Any element in the sentence, other than the subject, becomes emphatic when placed first.

Deceit or treachery he could never forgive.
So vast and rude, fretted by the action of nearly three thousand years, the fragments of this architecture may often seem, at first sight, like works of nature.

A subject coming first in its sentence may be emphatic, but hardly by its position alone. In the sentence,

32

> Great kings worshipped at his shrine,

the emphasis upon *kings* arises largely from its meaning and from the context. To receive special emphasis, the subject of a sentence must take the position of the predicate.

> Through the middle of the valley flowed a winding stream.

The principle that the proper place for what is to be made most prominent is the end applies equally to the words of a sentence, to the sentences of a paragraph, and to the paragraphs of a composition.

IV. A FEW MATTERS OF FORM

- **Headings.** Leave a blank line, or its equivalent in space, after the title or heading of a manuscript. On succeeding pages, if using ruled paper, begin on the first line.

- **Numerals.** Do not spell out dates or other serial numbers. Write them in figures or in Roman notation, as may be appropriate.

| August 9, 1918 | Chapter XII |
| Rule 3 | 352d Infantry |

- **Parentheses.** A sentence containing an expression in parenthesis is punctuated, outside of the marks of parenthesis, exactly as if the expression in parenthesis were absent. The expression within is punctuated as if it stood by itself, except that the final stop is omitted unless it is a question mark or an exclamation point.

I went to his house yesterday (my third attempt to see him), but he had left town.
He declares (and why should we doubt his good faith?) that he is now certain of success.

(When a wholly detached expression or sentence is parenthesized, the final stop comes before the last mark of parenthesis.)

- **Quotations.** Formal quotations, cited as documentary evidence, are introduced by a colon and enclosed in quotation marks.

The provision of the Constitution is: "No tax or duty shall be laid on articles exported from any state."

Quotations grammatically in apposition or the direct objects of verbs are preceded by a comma and enclosed in quotation marks.

> I recall the maxim of La Rochefoucauld, "Gratitude is a lively sense of benefits to come."

> Aristotle says, "Art is an imitation of nature."

Quotations of an entire line, or more, of verse, are begun on a fresh line and centred, but not enclosed in quotation marks.

> Wordsworth's enthusiasm for the Revolution was at first unbounded:

> Bliss was it in that dawn to be alive,

> But to be young was very heaven!

Quotations introduced by *that* are regarded as in indirect discourse and not enclosed in quotation marks.

> Keats declares that beauty is truth, truth beauty.

Proverbial expressions and familiar phrases of literary origin require no quotation marks.

> These are the times that try men's souls.

> He lives far from the madding crowd.

The same is true of colloquialisms and slang.

- **References.** In scholarly work requiring exact references, abbreviate titles that occur frequently, giving the full forms in an alphabetical list at the end. As a general practice, give the references in parenthesis or in footnotes, not in the body of the sentence. Omit the words *act, scene, line, book, volume, page,* except when referring by only one of them. Punctuate as indicated below.

In the second scene of the third act	In III.ii (still better, simply insert III.ii in parenthesis at the proper place in the sentence)
After the killing of Polonius, Hamlet is placed under guard (IV. ii. 14).	
2 *Samuel* i:17-27	*Othello* II.iii 264-267, III.iii. 155-161

- **Titles.** For the titles of literary works, scholarly usage prefers italics with capitalized initials. The usage of editors and publishers varies, some using italics with capitalized initials, others using Roman with capitalized initials and with or without quotation marks. Use italics (indicated in manuscript by underscoring), except in writing for a periodical that follows a different practice. Omit initial *A* or *The* from titles when you place the possessive before them.

> The *Iliad;* the *Odyssey; As You Like It; To a Skylark; The Newcomes; A Tale of Two Cities;* Dickens's *Tale of Two Cities.*

V. Words and Expressions Commonly Misused

(Many of the words and expressions here listed are not so much bad English as bad style, the commonplaces of careless writing. As illustrated under *Feature,* the proper correction is likely to be not the replacement of one word or set of words by another, but the replacement of vague generality by definite statement.)

- **All right.** Idiomatic in familiar speech as a detached phrase in the sense, "Agreed," or "Go ahead." In other uses better avoided. Always written as two words.

- **As good or better than.** Expressions of this type should be corrected by rearranging the sentence.

My opinion is as good or better than his.	My opinion is as good as his, or better (if not better).

- **As to whether.** *Whether* is sufficient; see under <u>Rule 13</u>.

- **Bid.** Takes the infinitive without *to.* The past tense is *bade.*

- **Case.** The *Concise Oxford Dictionary* begins its definition of this word: "instance of a thing's occurring; usual state of affairs." In these two senses, the word is usually unnecessary.

In many cases, the rooms were poorly ventilated.	Many of the rooms were poorly ventilated.
It has rarely been the case that any mistake has been made.	Few mistakes have been made.

See Wood, *Suggestions to Authors,* pp. 68-71, and Quiller-Couch, *The Art of Writing,* pp. 103-106.

- **Certainly.** Used indiscriminately by some speakers, much as others use *,very*[*] to intensify any and every statement. A mannerism of this kind, bad in speech, is even worse in writing.

- **Character.** Often simply redundant, used from a mere habit of wordiness.

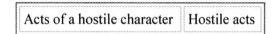

Acts of a hostile character	Hostile acts

- **Claim, vb.** With object-noun, means *lay claim to.* May be used with a dependent clause if this sense is clearly involved: "He claimed that he was the sole surviving heir." (But even here, "claimed to be" would be better.) Not to be used as a substitute for *declare, maintain,* or *charge.*

- **Compare.** To *compare to* is to point out or imply resemblances, between objects regarded as essentially of different order; to *compare with* is mainly to point out differences, between objects regarded as essentially of the same order. Thus life has been compared to a pilgrimage, to a drama, to a battle; Congress may be compared with the British Parliament. Paris has been compared to ancient Athens; it may be compared with modern London.

- **Clever.** This word has been greatly overused; it is best restricted to ingenuity displayed in small matters.

- **Consider.** Not followed by *as* when it means, "believe to be." "I consider him thoroughly competent." Compare, "The lecturer considered Cromwell first as soldier and second as administrator," where "considered" means "examined" or "discussed."

- **Dependable.** A needless substitute for *reliable, trustworthy.*

---

[*] Use this word sparingly. Where emphasis is necessary, use words strong in themselves.

- **Due to.** Incorrectly used for *through, because of,* or *owing to,* in adverbial phrases: "He lost the first game, due to carelessness." In correct use related as predicate or as modifier to a particular noun: "This invention is due to Edison;" "losses due to preventable fires."

- **Effect.** As noun, means *result;* as verb, means *to bring about, accomplish* (not to be confused with *affect,* which means "to influence").

  As noun, often loosely used in perfunctory writing about fashions, music, painting, and other arts: "an Oriental effect;" "effects in pale green;" "very delicate effects;" "broad effects;" "subtle effects;" "a charming effect was produced by." The writer who has a definite meaning to express will not take refuge in such vagueness.

- **Etc.** Not to be used of persons. Equivalent to *and the rest, and so forth,* and hence not to be used if one of these would be insufficient, that is, if the reader would be left in doubt as to any important particulars. Least open to objection when it represents the last terms of a list already given in full, or immaterial words at the end of a quotation.

  At the end of a list introduced by *such as, for example,* or any similar expression, *etc.* is incorrect.

- **Fact.** Use this word only of matters of a kind capable of direct verification, not of matters of judgment. That a particular event happened on a given date, that lead melts at a certain temperature, are facts. But such conclusions as that Napoleon was the greatest of modern generals, or that the climate of California is delightful, however incontestable they may be, are not properly facts.

  On the formula *the fact that,* see under Rule 13.

- **Factor.** A hackneyed word; the expressions of which it forms part can usually be replaced by something more direct and idiomatic.

His superior training was the great factor in his winning the match.	He won the match by being better trained.
Heavy artillery is becoming an increasingly important factor in deciding battles.	Heavy artillery is playing a larger and larger part in deciding battles.

- **Feature.** Another hackneyed word; like *factor** it usually adds nothing to the sentence in which it occurs.

A feature of the entertainment especially worthy of mention was the singing of Miss A.	(Better use the same number of words to tell what Miss A. sang, or if the programme has already been given, to tell something of how she sang.)

As a verb, in the advertising sense of *offer as a special attraction,* to be avoided.

- **Fix.** Colloquial in America for *arrange, prepare, mend.* In writing restrict it to its literary senses, *fasten, make firm or immovable,* etc.

- **He is a man who.** A common type of redundant expression; see <u>Rule 13</u>.

He is a man who is very ambitious.	He is very ambitious.
Spain is a country which I have always wanted to visit.	I have always wanted to visit Spain.

- **However.** In the meaning *nevertheless,* not to come first in its sentence or clause.

-

- A hackneyed word; the expressions of which it forms part can usually be replaced by something more direct and idiomatic.

The roads were almost impassable. However, we at last succeeded in reaching camp.	The roads were almost impassable. At last, however, we succeeded in reaching camp.

When *however* comes first, it means *in whatever way* or *to whatever extent.*

However you advise him, he will probably do as he thinks best.
However discouraging the prospect, he never lost heart.

- **Kind of.** Not to be used as a substitute for *rather* (before adjectives and verbs), or except in familiar style, for *something like* (before nouns). Restrict it to its literal sense: "Amber is a kind of fossil resin;" "I dislike that kind of notoriety." The same holds true of *sort of.*

- **Less.** Should not be misused for *fewer.*

He had less men than in the previous campaign.	He had fewer men than in the previous campaign.

Less refers to quantity, *fewer* to number. "His troubles are less than mine" means "His troubles are not so great as mine." "His troubles are fewer than mine" means "His troubles are not so numerous as mine." It is, however, correct to say, "The signers of the petition were less than a hundred, "where the round number, a hundred, is something like a collective noun, and *less* is thought of as meaning a less quantity or amount.

- **Line, along these lines.** *Line* in the sense of *course of procedure, conduct, thought,* is allowable, but has been so much overworked, particularly in the phrase *along these lines,* that a writer who aims at freshness or originality had better discard it entirely.

Mr. B. also spoke along the same lines.	Mr. B. also spoke, to the same effect.
He is studying along the line of French literature.	He is studying French literature.

- **Literal, literally.** Often incorrectly used in support of exaggeration or violent metaphor.

A literal flood of abuse	A flood of abuse
Literally dead with fatigue	Almost dead with fatigue (dead tired)

- **Lose out.** Meant to be more emphatic than *lose,* but actually less so, because of its commonness. The same holds true of *try out, win out, sign up, register up.* With a number of verbs, *out* and *up* form idiomatic combinations: *find out, run out, turn out, cheer up, dry up, make up,* and others, each distinguishable in meaning from the simple verb. *Lose out* is not.

- **Most.** Not to be used for *almost.*

Most everybody	Almost everybody
Most all the time	Almost all the time

- **Nature.** Often simply redundant, used like *character*[*].

Acts of a hostile nature	Hostile acts

Often vaguely used in such expressions as "a lover of nature;" "poems about nature." Unless more specific statements follow, the reader cannot tell whether the poems have to do with natural scenery, rural life, the sunset, the untracked wilderness, or the habits of squirrels.

---

[*]   Often simply redundant, used from a mere habit of wordiness.

- **Near by.** Adverbial phrase, not yet fully accepted as good English, though the analogy of *close by* and *hard by* seems to justify it. *Near,* or *near at hand,* is as good, if not better.

   Not to be used as an adjective; use *neighboring.*

- **Oftentimes, ofttimes.** Archaic forms, no longer in good use. The modern word is *often.*

- **One hundred and one.** Retain the *and* in this and similar expressions, in accordance with the unvarying usage of English prose from Old English times.

- **One of the most.** Avoid beginning essays or paragraphs with this formula, as, "One of the most interesting developments of modern science is, etc.;" "Switzerland is one of the most interesting countries of Europe." There is nothing wrong in this; it is simply threadbare and forcible-feeble.

- **People.** *The people* is a political term, not to be confused with *the public.* From the people comes political support or opposition; from the public comes artistic appreciation or commercial patronage.

   The word *people* is not to be used with words of number, in place of *persons.* If of "six people" five went away, how many "people" would be left?

- **Phase.** Means a stage of transition or development: "the phases of the moon;" "the last phase." Not to be used for *aspect* or *topic.*

Another phase of the subject	Another point (another question)

- **Possess.** Not to be used as a mere substitute for *have* or *own.*

He possessed great courage.	He had great courage (was very brave).
He was the fortunate possessor of	He owned

- **Respective, respectively.** These words may usually be omitted with advantage.

Works of fiction are listed under the names of their respective authors.	Works of fiction are listed under the names of their authors.
The one mile and two mile runs were won by Jones and Cummings respectively.	The one mile and two mile runs were won by Jones and by Cummings.

In some kinds of formal writing, as in geometrical proofs, it may be necessary to use *respectively,* but it should not appear in writing on ordinary subjects.

- **So.** Avoid, in writing, the use of *so* as an intensifier: "so good;" "so warm;" "so delightful."

On the use of *so* to introduce clauses, see Rule 4.

- **Sort of.** See under **Kind of.**

- **State.** Not to be used as a mere substitute for *say, remark.* Restrict it to the sense of *express fully or clearly,* as, "He refused to state his objections."

- **Student body.** A needless and awkward expression, meaning no more than the simple word *students.*

A member of the student body	A student
Popular with the student body	Liked by the students
The student body passed resolutions.	The students passed resolutions.

- **System.** Frequently used without need.

Dayton has adopted the commission system of government.	Dayton has adopted government by commission.
The dormitory system	Dormitories

- **Thanking you in advance.** This sounds as if the writer meant, "It will not be worth my while to write to you again." Simply write, "Thanking you," and if the favor which you have requested is granted, write a letter of acknowledgment.

- **They.** A common inaccuracy is the use of the plural pronoun when the antecedent is a distributive expression such as *each, each one, everybody, every one, many a man,* which, though implying more than one person, requires the pronoun to be in the singular. Similar to this, but with even less justification, is the use of the plural pronoun with the antecedent *anybody, any one, somebody, some one,* the intention being either to avoid the awkward "he or she," or to avoid committing oneself to either. Some bashful speakers even say, "A friend of mine told me that they, etc."

  Use *he* with all the above words, unless the antecedent is or must be feminine.

- **Very.** Use this word sparingly. Where emphasis is necessary, use words strong in themselves.

- **Viewpoint.** Write *point of view,* but do not misuse this, as many do, for *view* or *opinion.*

- **While.** Avoid the indiscriminate use of this word for *and, but,* and *although.* Many writers use it frequently as a substitute for *and* or *but,* either from a mere desire to vary the connective, or from uncertainty which of the two connectives is the more appropriate. In this use it is best replaced by a semicolon.

The office and salesrooms are on the ground floor, while the rest of the building is devoted to manufacturing.	The office and salesrooms are on the ground floor; the rest of the building is devoted to manufacturing.

Its use as a virtual equivalent of *although* is allowable in sentences where this leads to no ambiguity or absurdity.

> While I admire his energy, I wish it were employed in a better cause.

This is entirely correct, as shown by the paraphrase,

> I admire his energy; at the same time I wish it were employed in a better cause.

Compare:

While the temperature reaches 90 or 95 degrees in the daytime, the nights are often chilly.	Although the temperature reaches 90 or 95 degrees in the daytime, the nights are often chilly.

The paraphrase,

> The temperature reaches 90 or 95 degrees in the daytime; at the same time the nights are often chilly,

shows why the use of *while* is incorrect.

In general, the writer will do well to use *while* only with strict literalness, in the sense of *during the time that.*

46

- **Whom.** Often incorrectly used for *who* before *he said* or similar expressions, when it is really the subject of a following verb.

His brother, whom he said would send him the money	His brother, who he said would send him the money
The man whom he thought was his friend	The man who (that) he thought was his friend (whom he thought his friend)

- **Worth while.** Overworked as a term of vague approval and (with *not*) of disapproval. Strictly applicable only to actions: "Is it worth while to telegraph?"

His books are not worth while.	His books are not worth reading (not worth one's while to read; do not repay reading).

The use of *worth while* before a noun ("a worth while story") is indefensible.

- **Would.** A conditional statement in the first person requires *should,* not *would.*

I should not have succeeded without his help.

The equivalent of *shall* in indirect quotation after a verb in the past tense is *should,* not *would.*

He predicted that before long we should have a great surprise.

To express habitual or repeated action, the past tense, without *would,* is usually sufficient, and from its brevity, more emphatic.

Once a year he would visit the old mansion.	Once a year he visited the old mansion.

47

VI. WORDS OFTEN MISSPELLED

accidentally	formerly	privilege
advice	humorous	pursue
affect	hypocrisy	repetition
beginning	immediately	rhyme
believe	incidentally	rhythm
benefit	latter	ridiculous
challenge	led	sacrilegious
criticize	lose	seize
deceive	marriage	separate
definite	mischief	shepherd
describe	murmur	siege
despise	necessary	similar
develop	occurred	simile
disappoint	parallel	too
duel	Philip	tragedy
ecstasy	playwright	tries
effect	preceding	undoubtedly
existence	prejudice	until
fiery	principal	

Write *to-day, to-night, to-morrow* (but not *together*) with hyphen.
Write *any one, every one, some one, some time* (except the sense of *formerly*) as two words.

THE END

HOW TO
SPEAK AND WRITE
CORRECTLY

By
JOSEPH DEVLIN, M.A.

Edited by
THEODORE WATERS

Originally published by

THE CHRISTIAN HERALD
NEW YORK

CONTENTS

CHAPTER XI
SLANG
Origin. American slang. Foreign slang.

CHAPTER XII
WRITING FOR NEWSPAPERS
Qualification. Appropriate subjects. Directions.

CHAPTER XIII
CHOICE OF WORDS
Small words. Their importance. The Anglo-Saxon element.

CHAPTER XIV
ENGLISH LANGUAGE
Beginning. Different Sources. The present.

CHAPTER XV
MASTERS AND MASTERPIECES OF LITERATURE
Great authors. Classification. The world's best books.

INTRODUCTION

In the preparation of this little work the writer has kept one end in view, viz.: To make it serviceable for those for whom it is intended, that is, for those who have neither the time nor the opportunity, the learning nor the inclination, to peruse elaborate and abstruse treatises on Rhetoric, Grammar, and Composition. To them such works are as gold enclosed in chests of steel and locked beyond power of opening. This book has no pretension about it whatever,—it is neither a Manual of Rhetoric, expatiating on the dogmas of style, nor a Grammar full of arbitrary rules and exceptions. It is merely an effort to help ordinary, everyday people to express themselves in ordinary, everyday language, in a proper manner. Some broad rules are laid down, the observance of which will enable the reader to keep within the pale of propriety in oral and written language. Many idiomatic words and expressions, peculiar to the language, have been given, besides which a number of the common mistakes and pitfalls have been placed before the reader so that he may know and avoid them.

The writer has to acknowledge his indebtedness to no one in *particular*, but to all in *general* who have ever written on the subject.

The little book goes forth—a finger-post on the road of language pointing in the right direction. It is hoped that they who go according to its index will arrive at the goal of correct speaking and writing.

CHAPTER I

REQUIREMENTS OF SPEECH

Vocabulary—Parts of Speech—Requisites

It is very easy to learn how to speak and write correctly, as for all purposes of ordinary conversation and communication, only about 2,000 different words are required. The mastery of just twenty hundred words, the knowing where to place them, will make us not masters of the English language, but masters of correct speaking and writing. Small number, you will say, compared with what is in the dictionary! But nobody ever uses all the words in the dictionary or could use them did he live to be the age of Methuselah, and there is no necessity for using them.

There are upwards of 200,000 words in the recent editions of the large dictionaries, but the one-hundredth part of this number will suffice for all your wants. Of course you may think not, and you may not be content to call things by their common names; you may be ambitious to show superiority over others and display your learning or, rather, your pedantry and lack of learning. For instance, you may not want to call a spade a spade. You may prefer to call it a spatulous device for abrading the surface of the soil. Better, however, to stick to the old familiar, simple name that your grandfather called it. It has stood the test of time, and old friends are always good friends.

To use a big word or a foreign word when a small one and a familiar one will answer the same purpose, is a sign of ignorance. Great scholars and writers and polite speakers use simple words.

To go back to the number necessary for all purposes of conversation correspondence and writing, 2,000, we find that a great many people who pass in society as being polished, refined and educated use less, for they know less. The greatest scholar alive hasn't more than four thousand different words at his command, and he never has occasion to use half the number.

In the works of Shakespeare, the most wonderful genius the world has ever known, there is the enormous number of 15,000 different words, but almost 10,000 of them are obsolete or meaningless today.

Every person of intelligence should be able to use his mother tongue correctly. It only requires a little pains, a little care, a little study to enable one to do so, and the recompense is great.

Consider the contrast between the well-bred, polite man who knows how to choose and use his words correctly and the underbred, vulgar boor, whose language grates upon the ear and jars the sensitiveness of the finer feelings. The blunders of the latter, his infringement of all the canons of grammar, his absurdities and monstrosities of language, make his very presence a pain, and one is glad to escape from his company.

The proper grammatical formation of the English language, so that one may acquit himself as a correct conversationalist in the best society or be able to write and express his thoughts and ideas upon paper in the right manner, may be acquired in a few lessons.

It is the purpose of this book, as briefly and concisely as possible, to direct the reader along a straight course, pointing out the mistakes he must avoid and giving him such assistance as will enable him to reach the goal of a correct knowledge of the English language. It is not a Grammar in any sense, but a guide, a silent signal-post pointing the way in the right direction.

THE ENGLISH LANGUAGE IN A NUTSHELL

All the words in the English language are divided into nine great classes. These classes are called the Parts of Speech. They are Article, Noun, Adjective, Pronoun, Verb, Adverb, Preposition, Conjunction and Interjection. Of these, the Noun is the most important, as all the others are more or less dependent upon it. A Noun signifies the name of any person, place or thing, in fact, anything of which we can have either thought or idea. There are two kinds of Nouns, Proper and Common. Common Nouns are names which belong in common to a race or class, as *man, city*. Proper Nouns distinguish individual members of a race or class as *John, Philadelphia*. In the former case *man* is a name which belongs in common to the whole race of mankind, and *city* is also a name which is common to all large centres of population, but *John* signifies a particular individual of the race, while *Philadelphia* denotes a particular one from among the cities of the world.

Nouns are varied by Person, Number, Gender, and Case. Person is that relation existing between the speaker, those addressed and the subject under consideration, whether by discourse or correspondence. The Persons are *First, Second* and *Third* and they represent respectively the speaker, the person addressed and the person or thing mentioned or under consideration.

Number is the distinction of one from more than one. There are two numbers, singular and plural; the singular denotes one, the plural two or more. The plural is generally formed from the singular by the addition of *s* or *es*.

Gender has the same relation to nouns that sex has to individuals, but while there are only two sexes, there are four genders, viz., masculine, feminine, neuter and common. The masculine gender denotes all those of the male kind, the feminine gender all those of the female kind, the neuter gender denotes inanimate things or whatever is without life, and common gender is applied to animate beings, the sex of which for the time being is indeterminable, such as fish, mouse, bird, etc. Sometimes things which are without life as we conceive it and which, properly speaking, belong to the neuter gender, are, by a figure of speech called Personification, changed into either the masculine or feminine gender, as, for instance, we say of the sun, *He* is rising; of the moon, *She* is setting.

Case is the relation one noun bears to another or to a verb or to a preposition. There are three cases, the *Nominative*, the *Possessive* and the *Objective*. The nominative is the subject of which we are speaking or the agent which directs the action of the verb; the possessive case denotes possession, while the objective indicates the person or thing which is affected by the action of the verb.

An *Article* is a word placed before a noun to show whether the latter is used in a particular or general sense. There are but two articles, *a* or *an* and *the*.

An *Adjective* is a word which qualifies a noun, that is, which shows some distinguishing mark or characteristic belonging to the noun.

DEFINITIONS

A *Pronoun* is a word used for or instead of a noun to keep us from repeating the same noun too often. Pronouns, like nouns, have case, number, gender and person. There are three kinds of pronouns, *personal*, *relative* and *adjective*.

A *verb* is a word which signifies action or the doing of something. A verb is inflected by tense and mood and by number and person, though the latter two belong strictly to the subject of the verb.

An *adverb* is a word which modifies a verb, an adjective and sometimes another adverb.

A *preposition* serves to connect words and to show the relation between the objects which the words express.

A *conjunction* is a word which joins words, phrases, clauses and sentences together.

An *interjection* is a word which expresses surprise or some sudden emotion of the mind.

THREE ESSENTIALS

The three essentials of the English language are: *Purity*, *Perspicuity* and *Precision*.

By *Purity* is signified the use of good English. It precludes the use of all slang words, vulgar phrases, obsolete terms, foreign idioms, ambiguous expressions or any ungrammatical language whatsoever. Neither does it sanction the use of any newly coined word until such word is adopted by the best writers and speakers.

Perspicuity demands the clearest expression of thought conveyed in unequivocal language, so that there may be no misunderstanding whatever of the thought or idea the speaker or writer wishes to convey. All ambiguous words, words of double meaning and words that might possibly be construed in a sense different from that intended, are strictly forbidden. Perspicuity requires a style at once clear and comprehensive and entirely free from pomp and pedantry and affectation or any straining after effect.

Precision requires concise and exact expression, free from redundancy and tautology, a style terse and clear and simple enough to enable the hearer or reader to comprehend immediately the meaning of the speaker or writer. It forbids, on the one hand, all long and involved sentences, and, on the other, those that are too short and abrupt. Its object is to strike the golden mean in such a way as to rivet the attention of the hearer or reader on the words uttered or written.

CHAPTER II

ESSENTIALS OF ENGLISH GRAMMAR

Divisions of Grammar—Definitions—Etymology.

In order to speak and write the English language correctly, it is imperative that the fundamental principles of the Grammar be mastered, for no matter how much we may read of the best authors, no matter how much we may associate with and imitate the best speakers, if we do not know the underlying principles of the correct formation of sentences and the relation of words to one another, we will be to a great extent like the parrot, that merely repeats what it hears without understanding the import of what is said. Of course the parrot, being a creature without reason, cannot comprehend; it can simply repeat what is said to it, and as it utters phrases and sentences of profanity with as much facility as those of virtue, so by like analogy, when we do not understand the grammar of the language, we may be making egregious blunders while thinking we are speaking with the utmost accuracy.

DIVISIONS OF GRAMMAR

There are four great divisions of Grammar, viz.:

Orthography, *Etymology*, *Syntax*, and *Prosody*.

Orthography treats of letters and the mode of combining them into words.

Etymology treats of the various classes of words and the changes they undergo.

Syntax treats of the connection and arrangement of words in sentences.

Prosody treats of the manner of speaking and reading and the different kinds of verse.

The three first mentioned concern us most.

LETTERS

A *letter* is a mark or character used to represent an articulate sound. Letters are divided into *vowels* and *consonants*. A vowel is a letter which makes a distinct sound by itself. Consonants cannot be sounded without the aid of vowels. The vowels are *a, e, i, o, u*, and sometimes *w* and *y* when they do not begin a word or syllable.

SYLLABLES AND WORDS

A syllable is a distinct sound produced by a single effort of [Transcriber's note: 1-2 words illegible] shall, pig, dog. In every syllable there must be at least one vowel.

A word consists of one syllable or a combination of syllables.

Many rules are given for the dividing of words into syllables, but the best is to follow as closely as possible the divisions made by the organs of speech in properly pronouncing them.

THE PARTS OF SPEECH

ARTICLE

An *Article* is a word placed before a noun to show whether the noun is used in a particular or general sense.

There are two articles, *a* or *an* and *the*. *A* or *an* is called the indefinite article because it does not point put any particular person or thing but indicates the noun in its widest sense; thus, *a* man means any man whatsoever of the species or race.

The is called the definite article because it points out some particular person or thing; thus, *the* man means some particular individual.

NOUN

A *noun* is the name of any person, place or thing as *John, London, book*. Nouns are proper and common.

Proper nouns are names applied to *particular* persons or places.

Common nouns are names applied to a whole kind or species.

Nouns are inflected by *number, gender* and *case*.

Number is that inflection of the noun by which we indicate whether it represents one or more than one.

Gender is that inflection by which we signify whether the noun is the name of a male, a female, of an inanimate object or something which has no distinction of sex.

Case is that inflection of the noun which denotes the state of the person, place or thing represented, as the subject of an affirmation or question, the owner or possessor of something mentioned, or the object of an action or of a relation.

Thus in the example, "John tore the leaves of Sarah's book," the distinction between *book* which represents only one object and *leaves* which represent two or more objects of the same kind is called *Number*; the distinction of sex between *John*, a male, and *Sarah*, a female, and *book* and *leaves*, things which are inanimate and neither male nor female, is called *Gender*; and the distinction of state between *John*, the person who tore the book, and the subject of the affirmation, *Mary*, the owner of the book, *leaves* the objects torn, and *book* the object related to leaves, as the whole of which they were a part, is called *Case*.

ADJECTIVE

An *adjective* is a word which qualifies a noun, that is, shows or points out some distinguishing mark or feature of the noun; as, A *black* dog.

Adjectives have three forms called degrees of comparison, the *positive*, the *comparative* and the *superlative*.

The *positive* is the simple form of the adjective without expressing increase or diminution of the original quality: *nice*.

The *comparative* is that form of the adjective which expresses increase or diminution of the quality: *nicer*.

The *superlative* is that form which expresses the greatest increase or diminution of the quality: *nicest*.

or

An adjective is in the positive form when it does not express comparison; as, "A *rich* man."

An adjective is in the comparative form when it expresses comparison between two or between one and a number taken collectively, as, "John is *richer* than James"; "he is *richer* than all the men in Boston."

An adjective is in the superlative form when it expresses a comparison between one and a number of individuals taken separately; as, "John is the *richest* man in Boston."

Adjectives expressive of properties or circumstances which cannot be increased have only the positive form; as, A *circular* road; the *chief* end; an *extreme* measure.

Adjectives are compared in two ways, either by adding *er* to the positive to form the comparative and *est* to the positive to form the superlative, or by prefixing *more* to the positive for the comparative and *most* to the positive for the superlative; as, *handsome, handsomer, handsomest* or *handsome, more handsome, most handsome*.

Adjectives of two or more syllables are generally compared by prefixing more and most.

Many adjectives are irregular in comparison; as, Bad, worse, worst; Good, better, best.

PRONOUN

A *pronoun* is a word used in place of a noun; as, "John gave his pen to James and *he* lent it to Jane to write *her* copy with *it*." Without the pronouns we would have to write this sentence,—"John gave John's pen to James and James lent the pen to Jane to write Jane's copy with the pen."

There are three kinds of pronouns—Personal, Relative and Adjective Pronouns.

Personal Pronouns are so called because they are used instead of the names of persons, places and things. The Personal Pronouns are *I, Thou, He, She,* and *It,* with their plurals, *We, Ye* or *You* and *They.*

I is the pronoun of the first person because it represents the person speaking.

Thou is the pronoun of the second person because it represents the person spoken to.

He, She, It are the pronouns of the third person because they represent the persons or things of whom we are speaking.

Like nouns, the Personal Pronouns have number, gender and case. The gender of the first and second person is obvious, as they represent the person or persons speaking and those who are addressed. The personal pronouns are thus declined:

First Person.
M. or F.

	Sing.	*Plural.*
N.	I	We
P.	Mine	Ours
O.	Me	Us

Second Person.
M. or F.

	Sing.	*Plural.*
N.	Thou	You
P.	Thine	Yours
O.	Thee	You

Third Person.
M.

	Sing.	*Plural.*
N.	He	They
P.	His	Theirs
O.	Him	Them

Third Person.
F.

	Sing.	*Plural.*
N.	She	They
P.	Hers	Theirs
O.	Her	Them

Third Person.
Neuter.

	Sing.	*Plural.*
N.	It	They
P.	Its	Theirs
O.	It	Them

N. B.—In colloquial language and ordinary writing Thou, Thine and Thee are seldom used, except by the Society of Friends. The Plural form You is used for both the nominative and objective singular in the second person and Yours is generally used in the possessive in place of Thine.

The *Relative* Pronouns are so called because they relate to some word or phrase going before; as, "The boy *who* told the truth;" "He has done well, *which* gives me great pleasure."

Here *who* and *which* are not only used in place of other words, but *who* refers immediately to boy, and *which* to the circumstance of his having done well.

The word or clause to which a relative pronoun refers is called the *Antecedent*.

The Relative Pronouns are *who, which, that* and *what*.

Who is applied to persons only; as, "The man *who* was here."

Which is applied to the lower animals and things without life; as, "The horse *which* I sold." "The hat *which* I bought."

That is applied to both persons and things; as, "The friend *that* helps." "The bird *that* sings." "The knife *that* cuts."

What is a compound relative, including both the antecedent and the relative and is equivalent to *that which*; as, "I did what he desired," i. e. "I did *that which* he desired."

Relative pronouns have the singular and plural alike.

Who is either masculine or feminine; *which* and *that* are masculine, feminine or neuter; *what* as a relative pronoun is always neuter.

That and *what* are not inflected.

Who and *which* are thus declined:

Sing. and Plural		*Sing. and Plural*	
N.	Who	N.	Which
P.	Whose	P.	Whose
O.	Whom	O.	Which

Who, which and *what* when used to ask questions are called *Interrogative Pronouns.*

Adjective Pronouns partake of the nature of adjectives and pronouns and are subdivided as follows:

Demonstrative Adjective Pronouns which directly point out the person or object. They are *this, that* with their plurals *these, those,* and *yon, same* and *selfsame.*

Distributive Adjective Pronouns used distributively. They are *each, every, either, neither.*

Indefinite Adjective Pronouns used more or less indefinitely. They are *any, all, few, some, several, one, other, another, none.*

Possessive Adjective Pronouns denoting possession. They are *my, thy, his, her, its, our, your, their.*

N. B.—(The possessive adjective pronouns differ from the possessive case of the personal pronouns in that the latter can stand *alone* while the former *cannot.* "Who owns that book?" "It is *mine.*" You cannot say "it is *my,*"—the word book must be repeated.)

THE VERB

A *verb* is a word which implies action or the doing of something, or it may be defined as a word which affirms, commands or asks a question.

Thus, the words *John the table*, contain no assertion, but when the word *strikes* is introduced, something is affirmed, hence the word *strikes* is a verb and gives completeness and meaning to the group.

The simple form of the verb without inflection is called the *root* of the verb; *e. g. love* is the root of the verb,—"To Love."

Verbs are *regular* or *irregular, transitive* or *intransitive*.

A verb is said to be *regular* when it forms the past tense by adding *ed* to the present or *d* if the verb ends in *e*. When its past tense does not end in *ed* it is said to be *irregular*.

A *transitive* verb is one the action of which passes over to or affects some object; as "I struck the table." Here the action of striking affected the object table, hence struck is a transitive verb.

An *intransitive* verb is one in which the action remains with the subject; as *"I walk," "I sit," "I run."*

Many intransitive verbs, however, can be used transitively; thus, "I *walk* the horse;" *walk* is here transitive.

Verbs are inflected by *number, person, tense* and *mood.*

Number and *person* as applied to the verb really belong to the subject; they are used with the verb to denote whether the assertion is made regarding one or more than one and whether it is made in reference to the person speaking, the person spoken to or the person or thing spoken about.

TENSE

In their tenses verbs follow the divisions of time. They have *present tense, past tense* and *future tense* with their variations to express the exact time of action as to an event happening, having happened or yet to happen.

MOOD

There are four simple moods,—the *Infinitive*, the *Indicative*, the *Imperative* and the *Subjunctive*.

The Mood of a verb denotes the mode or manner in which it is used. Thus if it is used in its widest sense without reference to person or number, time or place, it is in the *Infinitive* Mood; as "To run." Here we are not told who does the running, when it is done, where it is done or anything about it.

When a verb is used to indicate or declare or ask a simple question or make any direct statement, it is in the *Indicative* Mood. "The boy loves his book." Here a direct statement is made concerning the boy. "Have you a pin?" Here a simple question is asked which calls for an answer.

When the verb is used to express a command or entreaty it is in the *Imperative* Mood as, "Go away." "Give me a penny."

When the verb is used to express doubt, supposition or uncertainty or when some future action depends upon a contingency, it is in the subjunctive mood; as, "If I come, he shall remain."

Many grammarians include a fifth mood called the *potential* to express *power, possibility, liberty, necessity, will* or *duty*. It is formed by means of the auxiliaries *may, can, ought* and *must*, but in all cases it can be resolved into the indicative or subjunctive. Thus, in "I may write if I choose," "may write" is by some classified as in the potential mood, but in reality the phrase *I may write* is an indicative one while the second clause, *if I choose,* is the expression of a condition upon which, not my liberty to write, depends, but my actual writing.

Verbs have two participles, the present or imperfect, sometimes called the *active* ending in *ing* and the past or perfect, often called the *passive,* ending in *ed* or *d.*

The *infinitive* expresses the sense of the verb in a substantive form, the participles in an adjective form; as "To rise early is healthful." "An early rising man." "The newly risen sun."

The participle in *ing* is frequently used as a substantive and consequently is equivalent to an infinitive; thus, "To rise early is healthful" and "Rising early is healthful" are the same.

The principal parts of a verb are the Present Indicative, Past Indicative and Past Participle; as:

Love	Loved	Loved

Sometimes one or more of these parts are wanting, and then the verb is said to be defective.

Present	Past	Passive Participle
Can	Could	(Wanting)
May	Might	"
Shall	Should	"
Will	Would	"
Ought	Ought	"

Verbs may also be divided into *principal* and *auxiliary*. A *principal* verb is that without which a sentence or clause can contain no assertion or affirmation. An *auxiliary* is a verb joined to the root or participles of a principal verb to express time and manner with greater precision than can be done by the tenses and moods in their simple form. Thus, the sentence, "I am writing an exercise; when I shall have finished it I shall read it to the class." has no meaning without the principal verbs *writing, finished read*; but the meaning is rendered more definite, especially with regard to time, by the auxiliary verbs *am, have, shall*.

There are nine auxiliary or helping verbs, viz., *Be, have, do, shall, will, may, can, ought*, and *must*. They are called helping verbs, because it is by their aid the compound tenses are formed.

TO BE

The verb *To Be* is the most important of the auxiliary verbs. It has eleven parts, viz., *am, art, is, are, was, wast, were, wert; be, being* and *been*.

VOICE

The *active voice* is that form of the verb which shows the Subject not being acted upon but acting; as, "The cat *catches* mice." "Charity *covers* a multitude of sins."

The *passive voice*: When the action signified by a transitive verb is thrown back upon the agent, that is to say, when the subject of the verb denotes the recipient of the action, the verb is said to be in the passive voice. "John was loved by his neighbors." Here John the subject is also the object affected by the loving, the action of the verb is thrown back on him, hence the compound verb *was loved* is said to be in the *passive voice*. The passive voice is formed by putting the perfect participle of any *transitive* verb with any of the eleven parts of the verb *To Be*.

CONJUGATION

The *conjugation* of a verb is its orderly arrangement in voices, moods, tenses, persons and numbers.

Here is the complete conjugation of the verb "Love"—*Active Voice*.

PRINCIPAL PARTS

Present	*Past*	*Past Participle*
Love	Loved	Loved

Infinitive Mood

To Love

Indicative Mood

PRESENT TENSE

	Sing.	*Plural*
1st person	I love	We love
2nd person	You love	You love
3rd person	He loves	They love

PAST TENSE

	Sing.	*Plural*
1st person	I loved	We loved
2nd person	You loved	You loved
3rd person	He loved	They loved

FUTURE TENSE

	Sing.	*Plural*
1st person	I shall love	They will love
2nd person	You will love	You will love
3rd person	He will love	We shall love

PRESENT PERFECT TENSE

	Sing.	*Plural*
1st person	I have loved	We have loved
2nd person	You have loved	You have loved
3rd person	He has loved	They have loved

PAST PERFECT TENSE

	Sing.	*Plural*
1st person	I had loved	We had loved
2nd person	You had loved	You had loved
3rd person	He had loved	They had loved

FUTURE PERFECT TENSE

	Sing.	*Plural*
1st person	I shall have loved	We shall have loved
2nd person	You will have loved	You will have loved
3rd person	He will have loved	They will have loved

Imperative Mood

(PRESENT TENSE ONLY)

	Sing.	*Plural*
2nd person	Love (you)	Love (you)

Subjunctive Mood

PRESENT TENSE

	Sing.	*Plural*
1st person	If I love	If we love
2nd person	If you love	If you love
3rd person	If he love	If they love

PAST TENSE

	Sing.	*Plural*
1st person	If I loved	If we loved
2nd person	If you loved	If you loved
3rd person	If he loved	If they loved

PRESENT PERFECT TENSE

	Sing.	*Plural*
1st person	If I have loved	If we have loved
2nd person	If you have loved	If you have loved
3rd person	If he has loved	If they have loved

PAST PERFECT TENSE

	Sing.	*Plural*
1st person	If I had loved	If we had loved
2nd person	If you had loved	If you had loved
3rd person	If he had loved	If they had loved

INFINITIVES

Present	*Perfect*
To love	To have loved

PARTICIPLES

Present	*Past*	*Perfect*
Loving	Loved	Having loved

CONJUGATION OF "To Love"

Passive Voice
Indicative Mood

PRESENT TENSE

	Sing.	*Plural*
1st person	I am loved	We are loved
2nd person	You are loved	You are loved
3rd person	He is loved	They are loved

PAST TENSE

	Sing.	*Plural*
1st person	I was loved	We were loved
2nd person	You were loved	You were loved
3rd person	He was loved	They were loved

FUTURE TENSE

	Sing.	*Plural*
1st person	I shall be loved	We shall be loved
2nd person	You will be loved	You will be loved
3rd person	He will be loved	They will be loved

PRESENT PERFECT TENSE

	Sing.	*Plural*
1st person	I have been loved	We have been loved
2nd person	You have been loved	You have been loved
3rd person	He has been loved	They have been loved

PAST PERFECT TENSE

	Sing.	*Plural*
1st person	I had been loved	We had been loved
2nd person	You had been loved	You had been loved
3rd person	He had been loved	They had been loved

FUTURE PERFECT TENSE

	Sing.	*Plural*
1st person	I shall have been loved	We shall have been loved
2nd person	You will have been loved	You will have been loved
3rd person	He will have been loved	They will have been loved

Imperative Mood

(PRESENT TENSE ONLY)

	Sing.	*Plural*
2nd person	Be (you) loved	Be (you) loved

Subjunctive Mood

PRESENT TENSE

	Sing.	*Plural*
1st person	If I be loved	If we be loved
2nd person	If you be loved	If you be loved
3rd person	If he be loved	If they be loved

PAST TENSE

	Sing.	*Plural*
1st person	If I were loved	If they were loved
2nd person	If you were loved	If you were loved
3rd person	If he were loved	If we were loved

72

PRESENT PERFECT TENSE

	Sing.	*Plural*
1st person	If I have been loved	If we have been loved
2nd person	If you have been loved	If you have been loved
3rd person	If he has been loved	If they have been loved

PAST PERFECT TENSE

	Sing.	*Plural*
1st person	If I had been loved	If we had been loved
2nd person	If you had been loved	If you had been loved
3rd person	If he had been loved	If they had been loved

INFINITIVES

Present	*Perfect*
To be loved	To have been loved

PARTICIPLES

Present	*Past*	*Perfect*
Being loved	Been loved	Having been loved

(N. B.—Note that the plural form of the personal pronoun, *you*, is used in the second person singular throughout. The old form *thou*, except in the conjugation of the verb "To Be," may be said to be obsolete. In the third person singular he is representative of the three personal pronouns of the third person, *He*, *She* and *It*.)

ADVERB

An *adverb* is a word which modifies a verb, an adjective or another adverb. Thus, in the example —"He writes *well*," the adverb shows the manner in which the writing is performed; in the examples —"He is remarkably diligent" and "He works very faithfully," the adverbs modify the adjective *diligent* and the other adverb *faithfully* by expressing the degree of diligence and faithfulness.

Adverbs are chiefly used to express in one word what would otherwise require two or more words; thus, *There* signifies in that place; *whence*, from what place; *usefully*, in a useful manner.

Adverbs, like adjectives, are sometimes varied in their terminations to express comparison and different degrees of quality.

Some adverbs form the comparative and superlative by adding *er* and *est*; as, *soon, sooner, soonest*.

Adverbs which end in *ly* are compared by prefixing *more* and *most*; as, *nobly, more nobly, most nobly*.

A few adverbs are irregular in the formation of the comparative and superlative; as, *well, better, best*.

PREPOSITION

A *preposition* connects words, clauses, and sentences together and shows the relation between them. "My hand is on the table" shows relation between hand and table.

Prepositions are so called because they are generally placed *before* the words whose connection or relation with other words they point out.

CONJUNCTION

A *conjunction* joins words, clauses and sentences; as "John *and* James." "My father and mother have come, *but* I have not seen them."

The conjunctions in most general use are *and, also; either, or; neither, nor; though, yet; but, however; for, that; because, since; therefore, wherefore, then; if, unless, lest.*

INTERJECTION

An *interjection* is a word used to express some sudden emotion of the mind. Thus in the examples, —"Ah! there he comes; alas! what shall I do?" *ah*, expresses surprise, and *alas,* distress.

Nouns, adjectives, verbs and adverbs become interjections when they are uttered as exclamations, as, *nonsense! strange! hail! away!* etc.

74

We have now enumerated the parts of speech and as briefly as possible stated the functions of each. As they all belong to the same family they are related to one another but some are in closer affinity than others. To point out the exact relationship and the dependency of one word on another is called *parsing* and in order that every etymological connection may be distinctly understood a brief resume of the foregoing essentials is here given:

The signification of the noun is *limited* to *one*, but to any *one* of the kind, by the *indefinite* article, and to some *particular* one, or some particular *number*, by the *definite* article.

Nouns, in one form, represent *one* of a kind, and in another, *any number* more than one; they are the *names of males*, or *females*, or of objects which are neither male nor female; and they represent the *subject* of an affirmation, a command or a question,—the *owner* or *possessor* of a thing,—or the *object* of an action, or of a relation expressed by a preposition.

Adjectives express the *qualities* which distinguish one person or thing from another; in one form they express quality *without comparison*; in another, they express comparison *between two*, or between *one* and a number taken collectively,—and in a third they express comparison between *one* and a *number* of others taken separately.

Pronouns are used in place of nouns; one class of them is used merely as the *substitutes* of *names*; the pronouns of another class have a peculiar *reference* to some *preceding words* in the *sentence*, of which they are the substitutes,—and those of a third class refer adjectively to the persons or things they represent. Some pronouns are used for both the *name* and the *substitute*; and several are frequently employed in *asking questions*.

Affirmations and *commands* are expressed by the verb; and different inflections of the verb express *number, person, time* and *manner*. With regard to *time*, an affirmation may be *present* or *past* or *future*; with regard to manner, an affirmation may be *positive* or *conditional*, it being doubtful whether the condition is fulfilled or not, or it being implied that it is not fulfilled;—the verb may express *command* or *entreaty*; or the sense of the verb may be expressed *without affirming* or *commanding*. The verb also expresses that an action or state *is* or *was* going on, by a form which is also used sometimes as a noun, and sometimes to qualify nouns.

Affirmations are *modified* by *adverbs*, some of which can be inflected to express different degrees of modification.

Words are joined together by *conjunctions*; and the various *relations* which one thing bears to another are expressed by *'prepositions. Sudden emotions* of the mind, and *exclamations* are expressed by *interjections*.

Some words according to meaning belong sometimes to one part of speech, sometimes to another. Thus, in "After a storm comes a *calm*," *calm* is a noun; in "It is a *calm* evening," *calm* is an adjective; and in "*Calm* your fears," *calm* is a verb.

The following sentence containing all the parts of speech is parsed etymologically:

"I now see the old man coming, but, alas, he has walked with much difficulty."

75

I, a personal pronoun, first person singular, masculine or feminine gender, nominative case, subject of the verb *see*.

now, an adverb of time modifying the verb *see*.

see, an irregular, transitive verb, indicative mood, present tense, first person singular to agree with its nominative or subject I.

the, the definite article particularizing the noun man.

old, an adjective, positive degree, qualifying the noun man.

man, a common noun, 3rd person singular, masculine gender, objective case governed by the transitive verb *see*.

coming, the present or imperfect participle of the verb "to come" referring to the noun man.

but, a conjunction.

alas, an interjection, expressing pity or sorrow.

he, a personal pronoun, 3rd person singular, masculine gender, nominative case, subject of verb has walked.

has walked, a regular, intransitive verb, indicative mood, perfect tense, 3rd person singular to agree with its nominative or subject *he*.

with, a preposition, governing the noun difficulty.

much, an adjective, positive degree, qualifying the noun difficulty.

difficulty, a common noun, 3rd person singular, neuter gender, objective case governed by the preposition *with*.

N.B.—*Much* is generally an adverb. As an adjective it is thus compared:

Positive	Comparative	Superlative
much	more	most

CHAPTER III

THE SENTENCE

Different Kinds—Arrangement of Words—Paragraph

A sentence is an assemblage of words so arranged as to convey a determinate sense or meaning, in other words, to express a complete thought or idea. No matter how short, it must contain one finite verb and a subject or agent to direct the action of the verb.

"Birds fly;" "Fish swim;" "Men walk;"—are sentences.

A sentence always contains two parts, something spoken about and something said about it. The word or words indicating what is spoken about form what is called the *subject* and the word or words indicating what is said about it form what is called the *predicate*.

In the sentences given, *birds*, *fish* and *men* are the subjects, while *fly*, *swim* and *walk* are the predicates.

There are three kinds of sentences, *simple*, *compound* and *complex*.

The *simple sentence* expresses a single thought and consists of one subject and one predicate, as, "Man is mortal."

A *compound sentence* consists of two or more simple sentences of equal importance the parts of which are either expressed or understood, as, "The men work in the fields and the women work in the household," or "The men work in the fields and the women in the household" or "The men and women work in the fields and in the household."

A *complex sentence* consists of two or more simple sentences so combined that one depends on the other to complete its meaning; as; "When he returns, I shall go on my vacation." Here the words, "when he returns" are dependent on the rest of the sentence for their meaning.

A *clause* is a separate part of a complex sentence, as "when he returns" in the last example.

A *phrase* consists of two or more words without a finite verb.

Without a finite verb we cannot affirm anything or convey an idea, therefore we can have no sentence.

Infinitives and participles which are the infinite parts of the verb cannot be predicates. "I looking up the street" is not a sentence, for it is not a complete action expressed. When we hear such an expression as "A dog running along the street," we wait for something more to be added, something more affirmed about the dog, whether he bit or barked or fell dead or was run over.

Thus in every sentence there must be a finite verb to limit the subject.

When the verb is transitive, that is, when the action cannot happen without affecting something, the thing affected is called the *object*.

Thus in "Cain killed Abel" the action of the killing affected Abel. In "The cat has caught a mouse," mouse is the object of the catching.

ARRANGEMENT OF WORDS IN A SENTENCE

Of course in simple sentences the natural order of arrangement is subject—verb—object. In many cases no other form is possible. Thus in the sentence "The cat has caught a mouse," we cannot reverse it and say "The mouse has caught a cat" without destroying the meaning, and in any other form of arrangement, such as "A mouse, the cat has caught," we feel that while it is intelligible, it is a poor way of expressing the fact and one which jars upon us more or less.

In longer sentences, however, when there are more words than what are barely necessary for subject, verb and object, we have greater freedom of arrangement and can so place the words as to give the best effect. The proper placing of words depends upon perspicuity and precision. These two combined give *style* to the structure.

Most people are familiar with Gray's line in the immortal *Elegy*—"The ploughman homeward plods his weary way." This line can be paraphrased to read 18 different ways. Here are a few variations:

```
Homeward the ploughman plods his weary way.
The ploughman plods his weary way homeward.
Plods homeward the ploughman his weary way.
His weary way the ploughman homeward plods.
Homeward his weary way plods the ploughman.
Plods the ploughman his weary way homeward.
His weary way the ploughman plods homeward.
His weary way homeward the ploughman plods.
The ploughman plods homeward his weary way.
The ploughman his weary way plods homeward.
```

and so on. It is doubtful if any of the other forms are superior to the one used by the poet. Of course his arrangement was made to comply with the rhythm and rhyme of the verse. Most of the variations depend upon the emphasis we wish to place upon the different words.

In arranging the words in an ordinary sentence we should not lose sight of the fact that the beginning and end are the important places for catching the attention of the reader. Words in these places have greater emphasis than elsewhere.

In Gray's line the general meaning conveyed is that a weary ploughman is plodding his way homeward, but according to the arrangement a very slight difference is effected in the idea. Some of the variations make us think more of the ploughman, others more of the plodding, and still others more of the weariness.

As the beginning and end of a sentence are the most important places, it naturally follows that small or insignificant words should be kept from these positions. Of the two places the end one is the more important, therefore, it really calls for the most important word in the sentence. Never commence a sentence with *And, But, Since, Because,* and other similar weak words and never end it with prepositions, small, weak adverbs or pronouns.

The parts of a sentence which are most closely connected with one another in meaning should be closely connected in order also. By ignoring this principle many sentences are made, if not nonsensical, really ridiculous and ludicrous. For instance: "Ten dollars reward is offered for information of any person injuring this property by order of the owner." "This monument was erected to the memory of John Jones, who was shot by his affectionate brother."

In the construction of all sentences the grammatical rules must be inviolably observed. The laws of concord, that is, the agreement of certain words, must be obeyed.

1.   The verb agrees with its subject in person and number. "I have," "Thou hast," (the pronoun *thou* is here used to illustrate the verb form, though it is almost obsolete), "He has," show the variation of the verb to agree with the subject. A singular subject calls for a singular verb, a plural subject demands a verb in the plural; as, "The boy writes," "The boys write."

The agreement of a verb and its subject is often destroyed by confusing (1) collective and common nouns; (2) foreign and English nouns; (3) compound and simple subjects; (4) real and apparent subjects.

(1) A collective noun is a number of individuals or things regarded as a whole; as, *class regiment.* When the individuals or things are prominently brought forward, use a plural verb; as The class *were* distinguished for ability. When the idea of the whole as a unit is under consideration employ a singular verb; as The regiment *was* in camp. (2) It is sometimes hard for the ordinary individual to distinguish the plural from the singular in foreign nouns, therefore, he should be careful in the selection of the verb. He should look up the word and be guided accordingly. "He was an *alumnus* of Harvard." "They were *alumni* of Harvard." (3) When a sentence with one verb has two or more subjects denoting different things, connected by *and,* the verb should be plural; as, "Snow and rain *are* disagreeable." When the subjects denote the same thing and are connected by *or* the verb should be singular; as, "The man or the woman is to blame." (4) When the same verb has more than one subject of different persons or numbers, it agrees with the most prominent in thought; as, "He, and not you, *is* wrong." "Whether he or I *am* to be blamed."

2.   Never use the past participle for the past tense nor *vice versa*. This mistake is a very common one. At every turn we hear "He done it" for "He did it." "The jar was broke" instead of broken. "He would have went" for "He would have gone," etc.

3.   The use of the verbs *shall* and *will* is a rock upon which even the best speakers come to wreck. They are interchanged recklessly. Their significance changes according as they are used with the first, second or third person. With the first person *shall* is used in direct statement to express a simple future action; as, "I shall go to the city to-morrow."

With the second and third persons *shall* is used to express a determination; as, "You *shall* go to the city to-morrow," "He *shall* go to the city to-morrow."

With the first person *will* is used in direct statement to express determination, as, "I will go to the city to-morrow." With the second and third persons *will* is used to express simple future action; as, "You *will* go to the city to-morrow," "He *will* go to the city to-morrow."

A very old rule regarding the uses of *shall* and *will* is thus expressed in rhyme:

```
        In the first person simply shall foretells,
        In will a threat or else a promise dwells.
Shall in the second and third does threat,
Will simply then foretells the future feat.
```

4. Take special care to distinguish between the nominative and objective case. The pronouns are the only words which retain the ancient distinctive case ending for the objective. Remember that the objective case follows transitive verbs and prepositions. Don't say "The boy who I sent to see you," but "The boy whom I sent to see you." *Whom* is here the object of the transitive verb sent. Don't say "She bowed to him and I" but "She bowed to him and me" since me is the objective case following the preposition *to* understood. "Between you and I" is a very common expression. It should be "Between you and me" since *between* is a preposition calling for the objective case.

5. Be careful in the use of the relative pronouns *who, which* and *that*. Who refers only to persons; which only to things; as, "The boy who was drowned," "The umbrella which I lost." The relative *that* may refer to both persons and things; as, "The man *that* I saw." "The hat *that* I bought."

6. Don't use the superlative degree of the adjective for the comparative; as "He is the richest of the two" for "He is the richer of the two." Other mistakes often made in this connection are (1) Using the double comparative and superlative; as, "These apples are much *more* preferable." "The most universal motive to business is gain." (2) Comparing objects which belong to dissimilar classes; as "There is no nicer *life* than a *teacher*." (3) Including objects in class to which they do not belong; as, "The fairest of her daughters, Eve." (4) Excluding an object from a class to which it does belong; as, "Caesar was braver than any ancient warrior."

7. Don't use an adjective for an adverb or an adverb for an adjective. Don't say, "He acted nice towards me" but "He acted nicely toward me," and instead of saying "She looked *beautifully*" say "She looked *beautiful*."

8. Place the adverb as near as possible to the word it modifies. Instead of saying, "He walked to the door quickly," say "He walked quickly to the door."

9. Not alone be careful to distinguish between the nominative and objective cases of the pronouns, but try to avoid ambiguity in their use.

The amusing effect of disregarding the reference of pronouns is well illustrated by Burton in the following story of Billy Williams, a comic actor who thus narrates his experience in riding a horse owned by Hamblin, the manager:

"So down I goes to the stable with Tom Flynn, and told the man to put the saddle on him."

"On Tom Flynn?"

"No, on the horse. So after talking with Tom Flynn awhile I mounted him."

"What! mounted Tom Flynn?"

"No, the horse; and then I shook hands with him and rode off."

"Shook hands with the horse, Billy?"

"No, with Tom Flynn; and then I rode off up the Bowery, and who should I meet but Tom Hamblin; so I got off and told the boy to hold him by the head."

"What! hold Hamblin by the head?"

"No, the horse; and then we went and had a drink together."

"What! you and the horse?"

"No, *me* and Hamblin; and after that I mounted him again and went out of town."

"What! mounted Hamblin again?"

"No, the horse; and when I got to Burnham, who should be there but Tom Flynn,—he'd taken another horse and rode out ahead of me; so I told the hostler to tie him up."

"Tie Tom Flynn up?"

"No, the horse; and we had a drink there."

"What! you and the horse?"

"No, me and Tom Flynn."

Finding his auditors by this time in a *horse* laugh, Billy wound up with: "Now, look here, — every time I say horse, you say Hamblin, and every time I say Hamblin you say horse: I'll be hanged if I tell you any more about it."

81

SENTENCE CLASSIFICATION

There are two great classes of sentences according to the general principles upon which they are founded. These are termed the *loose* and the *periodic*.

In the *loose* sentence the main idea is put first, and then follow several facts in connection with it. Defoe is an author particularly noted for this kind of sentence. He starts out with a leading declaration to which he adds several attendant connections. For instance in the opening of the story of *Robinson Crusoe* we read: "I was born in the year 1632 in the city of York, of a good family, though not of that country, my father being a foreigner of Bremen, who settled first at Hull; he got a good estate by merchandise, and leaving off his trade lived afterward at York, from whence he had married my mother, whose relations were named Robinson, a very good family in the country and from I was called Robinson Kreutznaer; but by the usual corruption of words in England, we are now called, nay, we call ourselves, and write our name Crusoe, and so my companions always called me."

In the periodic sentence the main idea comes last and is preceded by a series of relative introductions. This kind of sentence is often introduced by such words as *that, if, since, because*. The following is an example:

"That through his own folly and lack of circumspection he should have been reduced to such circumstances as to be forced to become a beggar on the streets, soliciting alms from those who had formerly been the recipients of his bounty, was a sore humiliation."

On account of its name many are liable to think the *loose* sentence an undesirable form in good composition, but this should not be taken for granted. In many cases it is preferable to the periodic form.

As a general rule in speaking, as opposed to writing, the *loose* form is to be preferred, inasmuch as when the periodic is employed in discourse the listeners are apt to forget the introductory clauses before the final issue is reached.

Both kinds are freely used in composition, but in speaking, the *loose*, which makes the direct statement at the beginning, should predominate.

As to the length of sentences much depends on the nature of the composition. However the general rule may be laid down that short sentences are preferable to long ones. The tendency of the best writers of the present day is towards short, snappy, pithy sentences which rivet the attention of the reader. They adopt as their motto *multum in parvo* (much in little) and endeavor to pack a great deal in small space. Of course the extreme of brevity is to be avoided. Sentences can be too short, too jerky, too brittle to withstand the test of criticism. The long sentence has its place and a very important one. It is indispensable in argument and often is very necessary to description and also in introducing general principles which require elaboration. In employing the long sentence the inexperienced writer should not strain after the heavy, ponderous type. Johnson and Carlyle used such a type, but remember, an ordinary mortal cannot wield the sledge hammer of a giant. Johnson and Carlyle were intellectual giants and few can hope to stand on the same literary pedestal. The tyro in composition should never seek after the heavy style. The best of all authors in the English language for style is Addison. Macaulay says: "If you wish a style learned, but not pedantic, elegant but not ostentatious, simple yet refined, you must give your days and nights to the volumes of Joseph Addison." The simplicity, apart from the beauty of Addison's writings causes us to reiterate the literary command—"Never use a big word when a little one will convey the same or a similar meaning."

Macaulay himself is an elegant stylist to imitate. He is like a clear brook kissed by the noon-day sun in the shining bed of which you can see and count the beautiful white pebbles. Goldsmith is another writer whose simplicity of style charms.

The beginner should study these writers, make their works his *vade mecum*, they have stood the test of time and there has been no improvement upon them yet, nor is there likely to be, for their writing is as perfect as it is possible to be in the English language.

Apart from their grammatical construction there can be no fixed rules for the formation of sentences. The best plan is to follow the best authors and these masters of language will guide you safely along the way.

THE PARAGRAPH

The paragraph may be defined as a group of sentences that are closely related in thought and which serve one common purpose. Not only do they preserve the sequence of the different parts into which a composition is divided, but they give a certain spice to the matter like raisins in a plum pudding. A solid page of printed matter is distasteful to the reader; it taxes the eye and tends towards the weariness of monotony, but when it is broken up into sections it loses much of its heaviness and the consequent lightness gives it charm, as it were, to capture the reader.

Paragraphs are like stepping-stones on the bed of a shallow river, which enable the foot passenger to skip with ease from one to the other until he gets across; but if the stones are placed too far apart in attempting to span the distance one is liable to miss the mark and fall in the water and flounder about until he is again able to get a foothold. 'Tis the same with written language, the reader by means of paragraphs can easily pass from one portion of connected thought to another and keep up his interest in the subject until he gets to the end.

Throughout the paragraph there must be some connection in regard to the matter under consideration,—a sentence dependency. For instance, in the same paragraph we must not speak of a house on fire and a runaway horse unless there is some connection between the two. We must not write consecutively:

"The fire raged with fierce intensity, consuming the greater part of the large building in a short time." "The horse took fright and wildly dashed down the street scattering pedestrians in all directions." These two sentences have no connection and therefore should occupy separate and distinct places. But when we say—"The fire raged with fierce intensity consuming the greater part of the large building in a short time and the horse taking fright at the flames dashed wildly down the street scattering pedestrians in all directions,"—there is a natural sequence, viz., the horse taking fright as a consequence of the flames and hence the two expressions are combined in one paragraph.

As in the case of words in sentences, the most important places in a paragraph are the beginning and the end. Accordingly the first sentence and the last should by virtue of their structure and nervous force, compel the reader's attention. It is usually advisable to make the first sentence short; the last sentence may be long or short, but in either case should be forcible. The object of the first sentence is to state a point *clearly*; the last sentence should *enforce* it.

It is a custom of good writers to make the conclusion of the paragraph a restatement or counterpart or application of the opening.

In most cases a paragraph may be regarded as the elaboration of the principal sentence. The leading thought or idea can be taken as a nucleus and around it constructed the different parts of the paragraph. Anyone can make a context for every simple sentence by asking himself questions in reference to the sentence. Thus—"The foreman gave the order"— suggests at once several questions; "What was the order?" "to whom did he give it?" "why did he give it?" "what was the result?" etc. These questions when answered will depend upon the leading one and be an elaboration of it into a complete paragraph.

If we examine any good paragraph we shall find it made up of a number of items, each of which helps to illustrate, confirm or enforce the general thought or purpose of the paragraph. Also the transition from each item to the next is easy, natural and obvious; the items seem to come of themselves. If, on the other hand, we detect in a paragraph one or more items which have no direct bearing, or if we are unable to proceed readily from item to item, especially if we are obliged to rearrange the items before we can perceive their full significance, then we are justified in pronouncing the paragraph construction faulty.

No specific rules can be given as to the construction of paragraphs. The best advice is,—Study closely the paragraph structure of the best writers, for it is only through imitation, conscious or unconscious of the best models, that one can master the art.

The best paragraphist in the English language for the essay is Macaulay, the best model to follow for the oratorical style is Edmund Burke and for description and narration probably the greatest master of paragraph is the American Goldsmith, Washington Irving.

A paragraph is indicated in print by what is known as the indentation of the line, that is, by commencing it a space from the left margin.

CHAPTER IV

FIGURATIVE LANGUAGE

Figures of Speech—Definitions and Examples —Use of Figures

In *Figurative Language* we employ words in such a way that they differ somewhat from their ordinary signification in commonplace speech and convey our meaning in a more vivid and impressive manner than when we use them in their every-day sense. Figures make speech more effective, they beautify and emphasize it and give to it a relish and piquancy as salt does to food; besides they add energy and force to expression so that it irresistibly compels attention and interest. There are four kinds of figures, viz.: (1) Figures of Orthography which change the spelling of a word; (2) Figures of Etymology which change the form of words; (3) Figures of Syntax which change the construction of sentences; (4) Figures of Rhetoric or the art of speaking and writing effectively which change the mode of thought.

We shall only consider the last mentioned here as they are the most important, really giving to language the construction and style which make it a fitting medium for the intercommunication of ideas.

Figures of Rhetoric have been variously classified, some authorities extending the list to a useless length. The fact is that any form of expression which conveys thought may be classified as a Figure.

The principal figures as well as the most important and those oftenest used are, *Simile, Metaphor, Personification, Allegory, Synechdoche, Metonymy, Exclamation, Hyperbole, Apostrophe, Vision, Antithesis, Climax, Epigram, Interrogation* and *Irony*.

The first four are founded on *resemblance*, the second six on *contiguity* and the third five, on *contrast*.

A *Simile* (from the Latin *similis*, like), is the likening of one thing to another, a statement of the resemblance of objects, acts, or relations; as "In his awful anger he was *like* the storm-driven waves dashing against the rock." A simile makes the principal object plainer and impresses it more forcibly on the mind. "His memory is like wax to receive impressions and like marble to retain them." This brings out the leading idea as to the man's memory in a very forceful manner. Contrast it with the simple statement—"His memory is good." Sometimes *Simile* is prostituted to a low and degrading use; as "His face was like a danger signal in a fog storm." "Her hair was like a furze-bush in bloom." "He was to his lady love as a poodle to its mistress." Such burlesque is never permissible. Mere *likeness*, it should be remembered, does not constitute a simile. For instance there is no simile when one city is compared to another. In order that there may be a rhetorical simile, the objects compared must be of different classes. Avoid the old *trite* similes such as comparing a hero to a lion. Such were played out long ago. And don't hunt for farfetched similes. Don't say—"Her head was glowing as the glorious god of day when he sets in a flambeau of splendor behind the purple-tinted hills of the West." It is much better to do without such a simile and simply say—"She had fiery red hair."

A *Metaphor* (from the Greek *metapherein*, to carry over or transfer), is a word used to *imply* a resemblance but instead of likening one object to another as in the *simile* we directly substitute the action or operation of one for another. The metaphor is a bolder and more lively figure than the simile. It is more like a picture and hence, the graphic use of metaphor is called "word-painting." It enables us to give to the most abstract ideas form, color and life. Our language is full of metaphors, and we very often use them quite unconsciously. For instance, when we speak of the *bed* of a river, the *shoulder* of a hill, the *foot* of a mountain, the *hands* of a clock, the *key* of a situation, we are using metaphors.

Don't use mixed metaphors, that is, different metaphors in relation to the same subject: "Since it was launched our project has met with much opposition, but while its flight has not reached the heights ambitioned, we are yet sanguine we shall drive it to success." Here our project begins as a *ship*, then becomes a *bird* and finally winds up as a *horse*.

Personification (from the Latin *persona*, person, and *facere*, to make) is the treating of an inanimate object as if it were animate and is probably the most beautiful and effective of all the figures.

"The mountains *sing* together, the hills *rejoice* and *clap* their hands."

"Earth *felt* the wound; and Nature from her seat,
Sighing, through all her works, gave signs of woe."

Personification depends much on a vivid imagination and is adapted especially to poetical composition. It has two distinguishable forms: (1) when personality is ascribed to the inanimate as in the foregoing examples, and (2) when some quality of life is attributed to the inanimate; as, a *raging* storm; an *angry* sea; a *whistling* wind, etc.

An *Allegory* (from the Greek *allos,* other, and *agoreuein,* to speak), is a form of expression in which the words are symbolical of something. It is very closely allied to the metaphor, in fact is a continued metaphor.

Allegory, metaphor and *simile* have three points in common,—they are all founded on resemblance. "Ireland is like a thorn in the side of England;" this is simile. "Ireland *is* a thorn in the side of England;" this is metaphor. "Once a great giant sprang up out of the sea and lived on an island all by himself. On looking around he discovered a little girl on another small island near by. He thought the little girl could be useful to him in many ways so he determined to make her subservient to his will. He commanded her, but she refused to obey, then he resorted to very harsh measures with the little girl, but she still remained obstate and obdurate. He continued to oppress her until finally she rebelled and became as a thorn in his side to prick him for his evil attitude towards her;" this is an allegory in which the giant plainly represents England and the little girl, Ireland; the implication is manifest though no mention is made of either country. Strange to say the most perfect allegory in the English language was written by an almost illiterate and ignorant man, and written too, in a dungeon cell. In the "Pilgrim's Progress," Bunyan, the itinerant tinker, has given us by far the best allegory ever penned. Another good one is "The Faerie Queen" by Edmund Spenser.

Synecdoche (from the Greek, *sun* with, and *ekdexesthai*, to receive), is a figure of speech which expresses either more or less than it literally denotes. By it we give to an object a name which literally expresses something more or something less than we intend. Thus: we speak of the world when we mean only a very limited number of the people who compose the world: as, "The world treated him badly." Here we use the whole for a part. But the most common form of this figure is that in which a part is used for the whole; as, "I have twenty head of cattle," "One of his *hands* was assassinated," meaning one of his men. "Twenty *sail* came into the harbor," meaning twenty ships. "This is a fine marble," meaning a marble statue.

Metonymy (from the Greek *meta*, change, and *onyma*, a name) is the designation of an object by one of its accompaniments, in other words, it is a figure by which the name of one object is put for another when the two are so related that the mention of one readily suggests the other. Thus when we say of a drunkard—"He loves the bottle" we do not mean that he loves the glass receptacle, but the liquor that it is supposed to contain. Metonymy, generally speaking, has, three subdivisions: (1) when an effect is put for cause or *vice versa*: as "*Gray hairs* should be respected," meaning old age. "He writes a fine hand," that is, handwriting. (2) when the *sign* is put for the *thing signified*; as, "The pen is mightier than the sword," meaning literary power is superior to military force. (3) When the *container* is put for the thing contained; as "The *House* was called to order," meaning the members in the House.

Exclamation (from the Latin *ex*, out, and *clamare*, to cry), is a figure by which the speaker instead of stating a fact, simply utters an expression of surprise or emotion. For instance when he hears some harrowing tale of woe or misfortune instead of saying,—"It is a sad story" he exclaims "What a sad story!"

Exclamation may be defined as the vocal expression of feeling, though it is also applied to written forms which are intended to express emotion. Thus in describing a towering mountain we can write "Heavens, what a piece of Nature's handiwork! how majestic! how sublime! how awe-inspiring in its colossal impressiveness!" This figure rather belongs to poetry and animated oratory than to the cold prose of every-day conversation and writing.

Hyperbole (from the Greek *hyper*, beyond, and *ballein*, to throw), is an exaggerated form of statement and simply consists in representing things to be either greater or less, better or worse than they really are. Its object is to make the thought more effective by overstating it. Here are some examples:—"He was so tall his head touched the clouds." "He was as thin as a poker." "He was so light that a breath might have blown him away." Most people are liable to overwork this figure. We are all more or less given to exaggeration and some of us do not stop there, but proceed onward to falsehood and downright lying. There should be a limit to hyperbole, and in ordinary speech and writing it should be well qualified and kept within reasonable bounds.

An *Apostrophe* (from the Greek *apo*, from, and *strephein*, to turn), is a direct address to the absent as present, to the inanimate as living, or to the abstract as personal. Thus: "O, illustrious Washington! Father of our Country! Could you visit us now!"

```
"My Country tis of thee—
 Sweet land of liberty,
 Of thee I sing."
```

"O! Grave, where is thy Victory, O! Death where is thy sting!" This figure is very closely allied to Personification.

Vision (from the Latin *videre*, to see) consists in treating the past, the future, or the remote as if present in time or place. It is appropriate to animated description, as it produces the effect of an ideal presence. "The old warrior looks down from the canvas and tells us to be men worthy of our sires."

This figure is much exemplified in the Bible. The book of Revelation is a vision of the future. The author who uses the figure most is Carlyle.

An *Antithesis* (from the Greek *anti*, against, and *tithenai*, to set) is founded on contrast; it consists in putting two unlike things in such a position that each will appear more striking by the contrast.

```
        "Ring out the old, ring in the new,
         Ring out the false, ring in the true."
```

"Let us be *friends* in peace, but *enemies* in war."

Here is a fine antithesis in the description of a steam engine—"It can engrave a seal and crush masses of obdurate metal before it; draw out, without breaking, a thread as fine as a gossamer; and lift up a ship of war like a bauble in the air; it can embroider muslin and forge anchors; cut steel into ribands, and impel loaded vessels against the fury of winds and waves."

Climax (from the Greek, *klimax*, a ladder), is an arrangement of thoughts and ideas in a series, each part of which gets stronger and more impressive until the last one, which emphasizes the force of all the preceding ones. "He risked truth, he risked honor, he risked fame, he risked all that men hold dear,—yea, he risked life itself, and for what?—for a creature who was not worthy to tie his shoe-latchets when he was his better self."

Epigram (from the Greek *epi*, upon, and *graphein*, to write), originally meant an inscription on a monument, hence it came to signify any pointed expression. It now means a statement or any brief saying in prose or poetry in which there is an apparent contradiction; as, "Conspicuous for his absence." "Beauty when unadorned is most adorned." "He was too foolish to commit folly." "He was so wealthy that he could not spare the money."

Interrogation (from the Latin *interrogatio*, a question), is a figure of speech in which an assertion is made by asking a question; as, "Does God not show justice to all?" "Is he not doing right in his course?" "What can a man do under the circumstances?"

Irony (from the Greek *eironcia*, dissimulation) is a form of expression in which the opposite is substituted for what is intended, with the end in view, that the falsity or absurdity may be apparent; as, "Benedict Arnold was an *honorable* man." "A Judas Iscariot never *betrays* a friend." "You can always *depend* upon the word of a liar."

Irony is cousin germain to *ridicule, derision, mockery, satire* and *sarcasm. Ridicule* implies laughter mingled with contempt; *derision* is ridicule from a personal feeling of hostility; *mockery* is insulting derision; *satire* is witty mockery; *sarcasm* is bitter satire and *irony* is disguised satire.

There are many other figures of speech which give piquancy to language and play upon words in such a way as to convey a meaning different from their ordinary signification in common every-day speech and writing. The golden rule for all is to *keep them in harmony with the character and purpose of speech and composition.*

CHAPTER V

PUNCTUATION

Principal Points—Illustrations—Capital Letters.

Lindley Murray and Goold Brown laid down cast-iron rules for punctuation, but most of them have been broken long since and thrown into the junk-heap of disuse. They were too rigid, too strict, went so much into *minutiae*, that they were more or less impractical to apply to ordinary composition. The manner of language, of style and of expression has considerably changed since then, the old abstruse complex sentence with its hidden meanings has been relegated to the shade, there is little of prolixity or long-drawn-out phrases, ambiguity of expression is avoided and the aim is toward terseness, brevity and clearness. Therefore, punctuation has been greatly simplified, to such an extent indeed, that it is now as much a matter of good taste and judgment as adherence to any fixed set of rules. Nevertheless there are laws governing it which cannot be abrogated, their principles must be rigidly and inviolably observed.

The chief end of punctuation is to mark the grammatical connection and the dependence of the parts of a composition, but not the actual pauses made in speaking. Very often the points used to denote the delivery of a passage differ from those used when the passage is written. Nevertheless, several of the punctuation marks serve to bring out the rhetorical force of expression.

The principal marks of punctuation are:

1.   The Comma [,]

2.   The Semicolon [;]

3.   The Colon [:]

4.   The Period [.]

5.   The Interrogation [?]

6.   The Exclamation [!]

7.   The Dash [—]

8.   The Parenthesis [( )]

9.   The Quotation ["   "]

There are several other points or marks to indicate various relations, but properly speaking such come under the heading of Printer's Marks, some of which are treated elsewhere.

Of the above, the first four may be styled the grammatical points, and the remaining five, the rhetorical points.

The *Comma*: The office of the Comma is to show the slightest separation which calls for punctuation at all. It should be omitted whenever possible. It is used to mark the least divisions of a sentence.

1. A series of words or phrases has its parts separated by commas:—"Lying, trickery, chicanery, perjury, were natural to him." "The brave, daring, faithful soldier died facing the foe." If the series is in pairs, commas separate the pairs: "Rich and poor, learned and unlearned, black and white, Mohammedan and Buddhist must pass through the same gate."

2. A comma is used before a short quotation: "It was Patrick Henry who said, 'Give me liberty or give me death.'"

3. When the subject of the sentence is a clause or a long phrase, a comma is used after such subject: "That he has no reverence for the God I love, proves his insincerity."

4. An expression used parenthetically should be inclosed by commas: "The old man, as a general rule, takes a morning walk."

5. Words in apposition are set off by commas: "McKinley, the President, was assassinated."

6. Relative clauses, if not restrictive, require commas: "The book, which is the simplest, is often the most profound."

7. In continued sentences each should be followed by a comma: "Electricity lights our dwellings and streets, pulls cars, trains, drives the engines of our mills and factories."

8. When a verb is omitted a comma takes its place: "Lincoln was a great statesman; Grant, a great soldier."

9. The subject of address is followed by a comma: "John, you are a good man."

10. In numeration, commas are used to express periods of three figures: "Mountains 25,000 feet high; 1,000,000 dollars."

The *Semicolon* marks a slighter connection than the comma. It is generally confined to separating the parts of compound sentences. It is much used in contrasts:

1. "Gladstone was great as a statesman; he was sublime as a man."

91

2. The Semicolon is used between the parts of all compound sentences in which the grammatical subject of the second part is different from that of the first: "The power of England relies upon the wisdom of her statesmen; the power of America upon the strength of her army and navy."

3. The Semicolon is used before words and abbreviations which introduce particulars or specifications following after, such as, *namely, as, e.g., vid., i.e., etc.*: "He had three defects; namely, carelessness, lack of concentration and obstinacy in his ideas." "An island is a portion of land entirely surrounded by water; as Cuba." "The names of cities should always commence with a capital letter; *e.g.*, New York, Paris." "The boy was proficient in one branch; viz., Mathematics." "No man is perfect; *i.e.*, free from all blemish."

The *Colon* except in conventional uses is practically obsolete.

1. It is generally put at the end of a sentence introducing a long quotation: "The cheers having subsided, Mr. Bryan spoke as follows:"

2. It is placed before an explanation or illustration of the subject under consideration: "This is the meaning of the term:"

3. A direct quotation formally introduced is generally preceded by a colon: "The great orator made this funny remark:"

4. The colon is often used in the title of books when the secondary or subtitle is in apposition to the leading one and when the conjunction *or* is omitted: "Acoustics: the Science of Sound."

5. It is used after the salutation in the beginning of letters: "Sir: My dear Sir: Gentlemen: Dear Mr. Jones:" etc. In this connection a dash very often follows the colon.

6. It is sometimes used to introduce details of a group of things already referred to in the mass: "The boy's excuses for being late were: firstly, he did not know the time, secondly, he was sent on an errand, thirdly, he tripped on a rock and fell by the wayside."

The *Period* is the simplest punctuation mark. It is simply used to mark the end of a complete sentence that is neither interrogative nor exclamatory.

1. After every sentence conveying a complete meaning: "Birds fly." "Plants grow." "Man is mortal."

2. In abbreviations: after every abbreviated word: Rt. Rev. T. C. Alexander, D.D., L.L.D.

3. A period is used on the title pages of books after the name of the book, after the author's name, after the publisher's imprint: *American Trails*. By Theodore Roosevelt. New York. Scribner Company.

The *Mark of Interrogation* is used to ask or suggest a question.

1. Every question admitting of an answer, even when it is not expected, should be followed by the mark of interrogation: "Who has not heard of Napoleon?"

2. When several questions have a common dependence they should be followed by one mark of interrogation at the end of the series: "Where now are the playthings and friends of my boyhood; the laughing boys; the winsome girls; the fond neighbors whom I loved?"

3. The mark is often used parenthetically to suggest doubt: "In 1893 (?) Gladstone became converted to Home Rule for Ireland."

The *Exclamation* point should be sparingly used, particularly in prose. Its chief use is to denote emotion of some kind.

1. It is generally employed with interjections or clauses used as interjections: "Alas! I am forsaken." "What a lovely landscape!"

2. Expressions of strong emotion call for the exclamation: "Charge, Chester, charge! On, Stanley, on!"

3. When the emotion is very strong double exclamation points may be used: "Assist him!! I would rather assist Satan!!"

The *Dash* is generally confined to cases where there is a sudden break from the general run of the passage. Of all the punctuation marks it is the most misused.

1. It is employed to denote sudden change in the construction or sentiment: "The Heroes of the Civil War,—how we cherish them." "He was a fine fellow—in his own opinion."

2. When a word or expression is repeated for oratorical effect, a dash is used to introduce the repetition: "Shakespeare was the greatest of all poets—Shakespeare, the intellectual ocean whose waves washed the continents of all thought."

3. The Dash is used to indicate a conclusion without expressing it: "He is an excellent man but—"

4. It is used to indicate what is not expected or what is not the natural outcome of what has gone before: "He delved deep into the bowels of the earth and found instead of the hidden treasure—a button."

93

5. It is used to denote the omission of letters or figures: "J—n J—s for John Jones; 1908-9 for 1908 and 1909; Matthew VII:5-8 for Matthew VII:5, 6, 7, and 8.

6. When an ellipsis of the words, *namely, that is, to wit,* etc., takes place, the dash is used to supply them: "He excelled in three branches—arithmetic, algebra, and geometry."

7. A dash is used to denote the omission of part of a word when it is undesirable to write the full word: He is somewhat of a r——l (rascal). This is especially the case in profane words.

8. Between a citation and the authority for it there is generally a dash: "All the world's a stage."—*Shakespeare.*

9. When questions and answers are put in the same paragraph they should be separated by dashes: "Are you a good boy? Yes, Sir.—Do you love study? I do."

Marks of Parenthesis are used to separate expressions inserted in the body of a sentence, which are illustrative of the meaning, but have no essential connection with the sentence, and could be done without. They should be used as little as possible for they show that something is being brought into a sentence that does not belong to it.

1. When the unity of a sentence is broken the words causing the break should be enclosed in parenthesis: "We cannot believe a liar (and Jones is one), even when he speaks the truth."

2. In reports of speeches marks of parenthesis are used to denote interpolations of approval or disapproval by the audience: "The masses must not submit to the tyranny of the classes (hear, hear), we must show the trust magnates (groans), that they cannot ride rough-shod over our dearest rights (cheers);" "If the gentleman from Ohio (Mr. Brown), will not be our spokesman, we must select another. (A voice,—Get Robinson)."

When a parenthesis is inserted in the sentence where no comma is required, no point should be used before either parenthesis. When inserted at a place requiring a comma, if the parenthetical matter relates to the whole sentence, a comma should be used before each parenthesis; if it relates to a single word, or short clause, no stop should come before it, but a comma should be put after the closing parenthesis.

The *Quotation marks* are used to show that the words enclosed by them are borrowed.

1. A direct quotation should be enclosed within the quotation marks: Abraham Lincoln said,—"I shall make this land too hot for the feet of slaves."

2. When a quotation is embraced within another, the contained quotation has only single marks: Franklin said, "Most men come to believe 'honesty is the best policy.'"

3. When a quotation consists of several paragraphs the quotation marks should precede each paragraph.

4. Titles of books, pictures and newspapers when formally given are quoted.

5. Often the names of ships are quoted though there is no occasion for it.

The *Apostrophe* should come under the comma rather than under the quotation marks or double comma. The word is Greek and signifies a turning away from. The letter elided or turned away is generally an *e*. In poetry and familiar dialogue the apostrophe marks the elision of a syllable, as "I've for I have"; "Thou'rt for thou art"; "you'll for you will," etc. Sometimes it is necessary to abbreviate a word by leaving out several letters. In such case the apostrophe takes the place of the omitted letters as "cont'd for continued." The apostrophe is used to denote the elision of the century in dates, where the century is understood or to save the repetition of a series of figures, as "The Spirit of '76"; "I served in the army during the years 1895, '96, '97, '98 and '99." The principal use of the apostrophe is to denote the possessive case. All nouns in the singular number whether proper names or not, and all nouns in the plural ending with any other letter than *s*, form the possessive by the addition of the apostrophe and the letter *s*. The only exceptions to this rule are, that, by poetical license the additional *s* may be elided in poetry for sake of the metre, and in the scriptural phrases "For goodness' sake." "For conscience' sake," etc. Custom has done away with the *s* and these phrases are now idioms of the language. All plural nouns ending in *s* form the possessive by the addition of the apostrophe only as boys', horses'. The possessive case of the personal pronouns never take the apostrophe, as ours, yours, hers, theirs.

CAPITAL LETTERS

Capital letters are used to give emphasis to or call attention to certain words to distinguish them from the context. In manuscripts they may be written small or large and are indicated by lines drawn underneath, two lines for SMALL CAPITALS and three lines for CAPITALS.

Some authors, notably Carlyle, make such use of Capitals that it degenerates into an abuse. They should only be used in their proper places as given in the table below.

1. The first word of every sentence, in fact the first word in writing of any kind should begin with a capital; as, "Time flies." "My dear friend."

2. Every direct quotation should begin with a capital; "Dewey said,—'Fire, when you're ready, Gridley!'"

3. Every direct question commences with a capital; "Let me ask you; 'How old are you?'"

4. Every line of poetry begins with a capital; "Breathes there a man with soul so dead?"

5. Every numbered clause calls for a capital: "The witness asserts: (1) That he saw the man attacked; (2) That he saw him fall; (3) That he saw his assailant flee."

6.   The headings of essays and chapters should be wholly in capitals; as, CHAPTER VIII —RULES FOR USE OF CAPITALS.

7.   In the titles of books, nouns, pronouns, adjectives and adverbs should begin with a capital; as, "Johnson's Lives of the Poets."

8.   In the Roman notation numbers are denoted by capitals; as, I II III V X L C D M—1, 2, 3, 5, 10, 50, 100, 500, 1000.

9.   Proper names begin with a capital; as, "Jones, Johnson, Caesar, Mark Antony, England, Pacific."

Such words as river, sea, mountain, etc., when used generally are common, not proper nouns, and require no capital. But when such are used with an adjective or adjunct to specify a particular object they become proper names, and therefore require a capital; as, "Mississippi River, North Sea, Alleghany Mountains," etc. In like manner the cardinal points north, south, east and west, when they are used to distinguish regions of a country are capitals; as, "The North fought against the South."

When a proper name is compounded with another word, the part which is not a proper name begins with a capital if it precedes, but with a small letter if it follows, the hyphen; as "Post-homeric," "Sunday-school."

10.   Words derived from proper names require a Capital; as, "American, Irish, Americanize."

In this connection the names of political parties, religious sects and schools of thought begin with capitals; as, "Republican, Democrat, Whig, Catholic, Presbyterian, Rationalists, Free Thinkers."

11.   The titles of honorable, state and political offices begin with a capital; as, "President, Chairman, Governor, Alderman."

12.   The abbreviations of learned titles and college degrees call for capitals; as, "LL.D., M.A., B.S.," etc. Also the seats of learning conferring such degrees as, "Harvard University, Manhattan College," etc.

13.   When such relative words as father, mother, brother, sister, uncle, aunt, etc., precede a proper name, they are written and printed with capitals; as, Father Abraham, Mother Eddy, Brother John, Sister Jane, Uncle Jacob, Aunt Eliza.

14.   The names applied to the Supreme Being begin with capitals: "God, Lord, Creator, Providence, Almighty, The Deity, Heavenly Father, Holy One." Also the designations of Biblical characters as "Lily of Israel, Rose of Sharon, Comfortress of the Afflicted, Prince of the Apostles, Star of the Sea," etc. Pronouns referring to God take capitals; as, "His work, The work of Him, etc."

15. Expressions used to designate the Bible or any particular division of it begin with a capital; as, "Holy Writ, The Sacred Book, Holy Book, God's Word, Gospel of St. Matthew, Seven Penitential Psalms."

16. Expressions based upon the Bible or in reference to Biblical characters begin with a capital: "Water of Life, Hope of Men, Scourge of Nations."

17. The names applied to the Evil One require capitals: "Beelzebub, Prince of Darkness, Satan, King of Hell, Devil, Incarnate Fiend, Tempter of Men, Father of Lies, Hater of Good."

18. Words of very special importance, especially those which stand out as the names of leading events in history, have capitals; as, "The Revolution, The Civil War, The Middle Ages, The Age of Iron," etc.

19. Terms which refer to great events in the history of the race require capitals; "The Flood, Magna Charta, Declaration of Independence."

20. The names of the days of the week and the months of the year and the seasons are commenced with capitals: "Monday, March, Autumn."

21. The Pronoun *I* and the interjection *O* always require the use of capitals. In fact all the interjections when uttered as exclamations commence with capitals: "Alas! he is gone." "Ah! I pitied him."

22. All *noms-de-guerre*, assumed names, as well as names given for distinction, call for capitals, as, "The Wizard of the North," "Paul Pry," "The Northern Gael," "Sandy Sanderson," "Poor Robin," etc.

23. In personification, that is, when inanimate things are represented as endowed with life and action, the noun or object personified begins with a capital; as, "The starry Night shook the dews from her wings." "Mild-eyed Day appeared," "The Oak said to the Beech—'I am stronger than you.'"

CHAPTER VI

LETTER WRITING

Principles of Letter-Writing—Forms—Notes

Many people seem to regard letter-writing as a very simple and easily acquired branch, but on the contrary it is one of the most difficult forms of composition and requires much patience and labor to master its details. In fact there are very few perfect letter-writers in the language. It constitutes the direct form of speech and may be called conversation at a distance. Its forms are so varied by every conceivable topic written at all times by all kinds of persons in all kinds of moods and tempers and addressed to all kinds of persons of varying degrees in society and of different pursuits in life, that no fixed rules can be laid down to regulate its length, style or subject matter. Only general suggestions can be made in regard to scope and purpose, and the forms of indicting set forth which custom and precedent have sanctioned.

The principles of letter-writing should be understood by everybody who has any knowledge of written language, for almost everybody at some time or other has necessity to address some friend or acquaintance at a distance, whereas comparatively few are called upon to direct their efforts towards any other kind of composition.

Formerly the illiterate countryman, when he had occasion to communicate with friends or relations, called in the peripatetic schoolmaster as his amanuensis, but this had one draw-back,—secrets had to be poured into an ear other than that for which they were intended, and often the confidence was betrayed.

Now, that education is abroad in the land, there is seldom any occasion for any person to call upon the service of another to compose and write a personal letter. Very few now-a-days are so grossly illiterate as not to be able to read and write. No matter how crude his effort may be it is better for any one to write his own letters than trust to another. Even if he should commence,—"deer fren, i lift up my pen to let ye no that i hove been sik for the past 3 weeks, hopping this will findye the same," his spelling and construction can be excused in view of the fact that his intention is good, and that he is doing his best to serve his own turn without depending upon others.

The nature, substance and tone of any letter depend upon the occasion that calls it forth, upon the person writing it and upon the person for whom it is intended. Whether it should be easy or formal in style, plain or ornate, light or serious, gay or grave, sentimental or matter-of-fact depend upon these three circumstances.

In letter writing the first and most important requisites are to be natural and simple; there should be no straining after effect, but simply a spontaneous out-pouring of thoughts and ideas as they naturally occur to the writer. We are repelled by a person who is stiff and labored in his conversation and in the same way the stiff and labored letter bores the reader. Whereas if it is light and in a conversational vein it immediately engages his attention.

The letter which is written with the greatest facility is the best kind of letter because it naturally expresses what is in the writer, he has not to search for his words, they flow in a perfect unison with the ideas he desires to communicate. When you write to your friend John Browne to tell him how you spent Sunday you have not to look around for the words, or study set phrases with a view to please or impress Browne, you just tell him the same as if he were present before you, how you spent the day, where you were, with whom you associated and the chief incidents that occurred during the time. Thus, you write natural and it is such writing that is adapted to epistolary correspondence.

There are different kinds of letters, each calling for a different style of address and composition, nevertheless the natural key should be maintained in all, that is to say, the writer should never attempt to convey an impression that he is other than what he is. It would be silly as well as vain for the common street laborer of a limited education to try to put on literary airs and emulate a college professor; he may have as good a brain, but it is not as well developed by education, and he lacks the polish which society confers. When writing a letter the street laborer should bear in mind that only the letter of a street-laborer is expected from him, no matter to whom his communication may be addressed and that neither the grammar nor the diction of a Chesterfield or Gladstone is looked for in his language. Still the writer should keep in mind the person to whom he is writing. All the laborer needs to know is the form of address and how to properly utilize his limited vocabulary to the best advantage. Here is the form for such a letter:

```
                    17 Second Avenue,
                       New York City.
                       January 1st, 1910.

Most Rev. P. A. Jordan,
     Archbishop of New York.

Most Rev. and dear Sir:—
     While sweeping the crossing at Fifth
Avenue and 50th street on last Wednesday
morning, I found the enclosed Fifty Dollar
Bill, which I am sending to you in the hope
that it may be restored to the rightful
owner.
     I beg you will acknowledge receipt and
should the owner be found I trust you will
notify me, so that I may claim some reward
for my honesty.
     I am, Most Rev. and dear Sir,

          Very respectfully yours,
                  Thomas Jones.
```

This letter, it is true, is different from that which he would send to Browne. Nevertheless it is simple without being familiar, is just a plain statement, and is as much to the point for its purpose as if it were garnished with rhetoric and "words of learned length and thundering sound."

Letters may be divided into those of friendship, acquaintanceship, those of business relations, those written in an official capacity by public servants, those designed to teach, and those which give accounts of the daily happenings on the stage of life, in other words, news letters.

Letters of friendship are the most common and their style and form depend upon the degree of relationship and intimacy existing between the writers and those addressed. Between relatives and intimate friends the beginning and end may be in the most familiar form of conversation, either affectionate or playful. They should, however, never overstep the boundaries of decency and propriety, for it is well to remember that, unlike conversation, which only is heard by the ears for which it is intended, written words may come under eyes other than those for whom they were designed. Therefore, it is well never to write anything which the world may not read without detriment to your character or your instincts. You can be joyful, playful, jocose, give vent to your feelings, but never stoop to low language and, above all, to language savoring in the slightest degree of moral impropriety.

Business letters are of the utmost importance on account of the interests involved. The business character of a man or of a firm is often judged by the correspondence. On many occasions letters instead of developing trade and business interests and gaining clientele, predispose people unfavorably towards those whom they are designed to benefit. Ambiguous, slip-shod language is a detriment to success. Business letters should be clear, concise, to the point and, above all, honest, giving no wrong impressions or holding out any inducements that cannot be fulfilled. In business letters, just as in business conduct, honesty is always the best policy.

Official letters are mostly always formal. They should possess clearness, brevity and dignity of tone to impress the receivers with the proper respect for the national laws and institutions.

Letters designed to teach or *didactic letters* are in a class all by themselves. They are simply literature in the form of letters and are employed by some of the best writers to give their thoughts and ideas a greater emphasis. The most conspicuous example of this kind of composition is the book on Etiquette by Lord Chesterfield, which took the form of a series of letters to his son.

News letters are accounts of world happenings and descriptions of ceremonies and events sent into the newspapers. Some of the best authors of our time are newspaper men who write in an easy flowing style which is most readable, full of humor and fancy and which carries one along with breathless interest from beginning to end.

The principal parts of a letter are (1) the *heading* or introduction; (2) the *body* or substance of the letter; (3) the *subscription* or closing expression and signature; (4) the *address* or direction on the envelope. For the *body* of a letter no forms or rules can be laid down as it altogether depends on the nature of the letter and the relationship between the writer and the person addressed.

There are certain rules which govern the other three features and which custom has sanctioned. Every one should be acquainted with these rules.

THE HEADING

The *Heading* has three parts, viz., the name of the place, the date of writing and the designation of the person or persons addressed; thus:

```
                    73 New Street,
                      Newark, N. J.,
                    February 1st, 1910.
Messr. Ginn and Co.,
     New York
Gentlemen:
```

The name of the place should never be omitted; in cities, street and number should always be given, and except when the city is large and very conspicuous, so that there can be no question as to its identity with another of the same or similar name, the abbreviation of the State should be appended, as in the above, Newark, N. J. There is another Newark in the State of Ohio. Owing to failure to comply with this rule many letters go astray. The *date* should be on every letter, especially business letters. The date should never be put at the bottom in a business letter, but in friendly letters this may be done. The *designation* of the person or persons addressed differs according to the relations of the correspondents. Letters of friendship may begin in many ways according to the degrees of friendship or intimacy. Thus:

```
My dear Wife:
My dear Husband:
My dear Friend:
My darling Mother:
My dearest Love:
Dear Aunt:
Dear Uncle:
Dear George: etc.
```

To mark a lesser degree of intimacy such formal designations as the following may be employed:

```
Dear Sir:
My dear Sir:
Dear Mr. Smith:
Dear Madam: etc.
```

For clergymen who have the degree of Doctor of Divinity, the designation is as follows:

```
Rev. Alban Johnson, D. D.
My dear Sir: or Rev. and dear Sir: or more familiarly
Dear Dr. Johnson:
```

Bishops of the Roman and Anglican Communions are addressed as *Right Reverend.*

```
The Rt. Rev., the Bishop of Long Island. or
The Rt. Rev. Frederick Burgess, Bishop of Long Island.
Rt. Rev. and dear Sir:
```

The title of the Governor of a State or territory and of the President of the United States is *Excellency.* However, *Honorable* is more commonly applied to Governors:—

```
His Excellency, William Howard Taft,
    President of the United States.

Sir:—

His Excellency, Charles Evans Hughes,
    Governor of the State of New York.

Sir:—

Honorable Franklin Fort,
    Governor of New Jersey.

Sir:—
```

The general salutation for Officers of the Army and Navy is *Sir.* The rank and station should be indicated in full at the head of the letter, thus:

```
General Joseph Thompson,
    Commanding the Seventh Infantry.

Sir:

Rear Admiral Robert Atkinson,
    Commanding the Atlantic Squadron.

Sir:
```

The title of officers of the Civil Government is Honorable and they are addressed as *Sir.*

```
Hon. Nelson Duncan,
    Senator from Ohio.

Sir:
```

```
Hon. Norman Wingfield,
   Secretary of the Treasury.

Sir:

Hon. Rupert Gresham,
   Mayor of New York.

Sir:
```

Presidents and Professors of Colleges and Universities are generally addressed as *Sir* or *Dear Sir*.

```
Professor Ferguson Jenks,
   President of ......... University.

Sir: or Dear Sir:
```

Presidents of Societies and Associations are treated as business men and addressed as *Sir* or *Dear Sir*.

```
   Mr. Joseph Banks,
      President of the Night Owls.

   Dear Sir: or Sir:
```

Doctors of Medicine are addressed as *Sir: My dear Sir: Dear Sir:* and more familiarly My dear Dr: or Dear Dr: as

```
   Ryerson Pitkin, M. D.
   Sir:
   Dear Sir:
   My dear Dr:
```

Ordinary people with no degrees or titles are addressed as Mr. and Mrs. and are designed Dear Sir: Dear Madam: and an unmarried woman of any age is addressed on the envelope as Miss So-and-so, but always designed in the letter as

```
   Dear Madam:
```

The plural of Mr. as in addressing a firm is *Messrs*, and the corresponding salutation is *Dear Sirs: or Gentlemen:*

In England *Esq.* is used for *Mr.* as a mark of slight superiority and in this country it is sometimes used, but it is practically obsolete. Custom is against it and American sentiment as well. If it is used it should be only applied to lawyers and justices of the peace.

SUBSCRIPTION

The *Subscription* or ending of a letter consists of the term of respect or affection and the signature. The term depends upon the relation of the person addressed. Letters of friendship can close with such expressions as:

```
Yours lovingly,
Yours affectionately,
Devotedly yours,
Ever yours, etc.
```

as between husbands and wives or between lovers. Such gushing terminations as Your Own Darling, Your own Dovey and other pet and silly endings should be avoided, as they denote shallowness. Love can be strongly expressed without dipping into the nonsensical and the farcical.

Formal expressions of Subscription are:

```
Yours Sincerely,
Yours truly,
Respectfully yours,
```

and the like, and these may be varied to denote the exact bearing or attitude the writer wishes to assume to the person addressed: as,

```
Very sincerely yours,
Very respectfully yours,
With deep respect yours,
Yours very truly, etc.
```

Such elaborate endings as

```
    "In the meantime with the highest respect, I am yours to
command,"
    "I have the honor to be, Sir, Your humble Servant,"
    "With great expression of esteem, I am Sincerely yours,"
    "Believe me, my dear Sir, Ever faithfully yours,"
```

are condemned as savoring too much of affectation.

It is better to finish formal letters without any such qualifying remarks. If you are writing to Mr. Ryan to tell him that you have a house for sale, after describing the house and stating the terms simply sign yourself

```
Your obedient Servant
Yours very truly,
Yours with respect,
  James Wilson.
```

Don't say you have the honor to be anything or ask him to believe anything, all you want to tell him is that you have a house for sale and that you are sincere, or hold him in respect as a prospective customer.

Don't abbreviate the signature as: *Y'rs Resp'fly* and always make your sex obvious. Write plainly

```
Yours truly,
John Field
```

and not *J. Field*, so that the person to whom you send it may not take you for *Jane Field*.

It is always best to write the first name in full. Married women should prefix *Mrs.* to their names, as

```
Very sincerely yours,
Mrs. Theodore Watson.
```

If you are sending a letter acknowledging a compliment or some kindness done you may say, *Yours gratefully,* or *Yours very gratefully,* in proportion to the act of kindness received.

It is not customary to sign letters of degrees or titles after your name, except you are a lord, earl or duke and only known by the title, but as we have no such titles in America it is unnecessary to bring this matter into consideration. Don't sign yourself,

```
        Sincerely yours,
          Obadiah Jackson, M.A. or L.L. D.
```

If you're an M. A. or an L.L. D. people generally know it without your sounding your own trumpet. Many people, and especially clergymen, are fond of flaunting after their names degrees they have received *honoris causa*, that is, degrees as a mark of honor, without examination. Such degrees should be kept in the background. Many a deadhead has these degrees which he could never have earned by brain work.

Married women whose husbands are alive may sign the husband's name with the prefix *Mrs:* thus,

```
Yours sincerely,
Mrs. William Southey.
```

but when the husband is dead the signature should be—

```
Yours sincerely,
Mrs. Sarah Southey.
```

So when we receive a letter from a woman we are enabled to tell whether she has a husband living or is a widow. A woman separated from her husband but not a *divorcee* should *not* sign his name.

ADDRESS

The *address* of a letter consists of the name, the title and the residence.

```
Mr. Hugh Black,
    112 Southgate Street,
      Altoona,
              Pa.
```

Intimate friends have often familiar names for each other, such as pet names, nicknames, etc., which they use in the freedom of conversation, but such names should never, under any circumstances, appear on the envelope. The subscription on the envelope should be always written with propriety and correctness and as if penned by an entire stranger. The only difficulty in the envelope inscription is the title. Every man is entitled to *Mr.* and every lady to *Mrs.* and every unmarried lady to *Miss*. Even a boy is entitled to *Master*. When more than one is addressed the title is *Messrs. Mesdames* is sometimes written of women. If the person addressed has a title it is courteous to use it, but titles never must be duplicated. Thus, we can write

```
Robert Stitt, M. D., but never
Dr. Robert Stitt, M. D, or
Mr. Robert Stitt, M. D.
```

In writing to a medical doctor it is well to indicate his profession by the letters M. D. so as to differentiate him from a D. D. It is better to write Robert Stitt, M. D., than Dr. Robert Stitt.

In the case of clergymen the prefix Rev. is retained even when they have other titles; as

```
Rev. Tracy Tooke, LL. D.
```

When a person has more titles than one it is customary to only give him the leading one. Thus instead of writing Rev. Samuel MacComb, B. A., M. A., B. Sc., Ph. D., LL. D., D. D. the form employed is Rev. Samuel MacComb, LL. D. LL. D. is appended in preference to D. D. because in most cases the "Rev." implies a "D. D." while comparatively few with the prefix "Rev." are entitled to "LL. D."

In the case of *Honorables* such as Governors, Judges, Members of Congress, and others of the Civil Government the prefix "Hon." does away with *Mr.* and *Esq.* Thus we write Hon. Josiah Snifkins, not Hon. Mr. Josiah Snifkins or Hon. Josiah Snifkins, Esq. Though this prefix *Hon.* is also often applied to Governors they should be addressed as Excellency. For instance:

```
His Excellency,
    Charles E. Hughes,
                Albany,
                   N. Y.
```

In writing to the President the superscription on the envelope should be

```
      To the President,
        Executive Mansion,
           Washington, D. C.
```

Professional men such as doctors and lawyers as well as those having legitimately earned College Degrees may be addressed on the envelopes by their titles, as

```
      Jonathan Janeway, M. D.
      Hubert Houston, B. L.
      Matthew Marks, M. A., etc.
```

The residence of the person addressed should be plainly written out in full. The street and numbers should be given and the city or town written very legibly. If the abbreviation of the State is liable to be confounded or confused with that of another then the full name of the State should be written. In writing the residence on the envelope, instead of putting it all in one line as is done at the head of a letter, each item of the residence forms a separate line. Thus,

```
      Liberty,
        Sullivan County,
               New York.

      215 Minna St.,
        San Francisco,
               California.
```

There should be left a space for the postage stamp in the upper right hand corner. The name and title should occupy a line that is about central between the top of the envelope and the bottom. The name should neither be too much to right or left but located in the centre, the beginning and end at equal distances from either end.

In writing to large business concerns which are well known or to public or city officials it is sometimes customary to leave out number and street. Thus,

```
      Messrs. Seigel, Cooper Co.,
                New York City,

      Hon. William J. Gaynor,
                New York City.
```

NOTES

Notes may be regarded as letters in miniature confined chiefly to invitations, acceptances, regrets and introductions, and modern etiquette tends towards informality in their composition. Card etiquette, in fact, has taken the place of ceremonious correspondence and informal notes are now the rule. Invitations to dinner and receptions are now mostly written on cards. "Regrets" are sent back on visiting cards with just the one word *"Regrets"* plainly written thereon. Often on cards and notes of invitation we find the letters R. S. V. P. at the bottom. These letters stand for the French *repondez s'il vous plait*, which means "Reply, if you please," but there is no necessity to put this on an invitation card as every well-bred person knows that a reply is expected. In writing notes to young ladies of the same family it should be noted that the eldest daughter of the house is entitled to the designation *Miss*. Thus if there are three daughters in the Thompson family Martha, the eldest, Susan and Jemina, Martha is addressed as *Miss* Thompson and the other two as *Miss* Susan Thompson and *Miss* Jemina Thompson respectively.

Don't write the word *addressed* on the envelope of a note.

Don't *seal* a note delivered by a friend.

Don't write a note on a postal card.

Here are a few common forms:—

FORMAL INVITATIONS

```
    Mr. and Mrs. Henry Wagstaff request the
honor of Mr. McAdoo's presence on Friday
evening, June 15th, at 8 o'clock to meet the
Governor of the Fort.
        19 Woodbine Terrace
                June 8th, 1910.
```

This is an invitation to a formal reception calling for evening dress. Here is Mr. McAdoo's reply in the third person:—

```
    Mr. McAdoo presents his compliments to
Mr. and Mrs. Henry Wagstaff and accepts with
great pleasure their invitation to meet the
Governor of the Fort on the evening of June
fifteenth.
    215 Beacon Street,
        June 10th, 1910.
```

Here is how Mr. McAdoo might decline the invitation:—

```
    Mr. McAdoo regrets that owing to a prior
engagement he must forego the honor of paying
his respects to Mr. and Mrs. Wagstaff and the
Governor of the Fort on the evening of June
fifteenth.
    215 Beacon St.,
        June 10th, 1910.
```

Here is a note addressed, say to Mr. Jeremiah Reynolds.

```
    Mr. and Mrs. Oldham at home on Wednesday
```

evening October ninth from seven to eleven.
21 Ashland Avenue,
October 5th.

Mr. Reynolds makes reply:—

Mr. Reynolds accepts with high appreciation
the honor of Mr. and Mrs. Oldham's invitation
for Wednesday evening October ninth.
Windsor Hotel
October 7th

or

Mr. Reynolds regrets that his duties render
it impossible for him to accept Mr. and Mrs.
Oldham's kind invitation for the evening of
October ninth.
Windsor Hotel,
October 7th,

Sometimes less informal invitations are sent on small specially designed note paper in which the first person takes the place of the third. Thus

360 Pine St.,
Dec. 11th, 1910.
Dear Mr. Saintsbury:
Mr. Johnson and I should be much pleased to
have you dine with us and a few friends next
Thursday, the fifteenth, at half past seven.
Yours sincerely,
Emma Burnside.

Mr. Saintsbury's reply:

57 Carlyle Strand
Dec. 13th, 1910.
Dear Mrs. Burnside:
Let me accept very appreciatively your
invitation to dine with Mr. Burnside and you
on next Thursday, the fifteenth, at half past
seven.
Yours sincerely,
Henry Saintsbury.
Mrs. Alexander Burnside.

NOTES OF INTRODUCTION

Notes of introduction should be very circumspect as the writers are in reality vouching for those whom they introduce. Here is a specimen of such a note.

```
                   603 Lexington Ave.,
                      New York City,
                       June 15th, 1910.

Rev. Cyrus C. Wiley, D. D.,
              Newark, N. J.
My dear Dr. Wiley:
                  I take the liberty of
presenting to you my friend, Stacy Redfern,
M. D., a young practitioner, who is anxious
to locate in Newark. I have known him many
years and can vouch for his integrity and
professional standing. Any courtesy and
kindness which you may show him will be very
much appreciated by me.
                  Very sincerely yours,
                      Franklin Jewett.
```

CHAPTER VII

ERRORS

Mistakes—Slips of Authors—Examples and Corrections—Errors of Redundancy.

In the following examples the word or words in parentheses are uncalled for and should be omitted:

1.	Fill the glass (full).

2.	They appeared to be talking (together) on private affairs.

3.	I saw the boy and his sister (both) in the garden.

4.	He went into the country last week and returned (back) yesterday.

5.	The subject (matter) of his discourse was excellent.

6.	You need not wonder that the (subject) matter of his discourse was excellent; it was taken from the Bible.

7.	They followed (after) him, but could not overtake him.

8.	The same sentiments may be found throughout (the whole of) the book.

9.	I was very ill every day (of my life) last week.

10.	That was the (sum and) substance of his discourse.

11.	He took wine and water and mixed them (both) together.

12.	He descended (down) the steps to the cellar.

13.	He fell (down) from the top of the house.

14.	I hope you will return (again) soon.

15.	The things he took away he restored (again).

16.	The thief who stole my watch was compelled to restore it (back again).

17.	It is equally (the same) to me whether I have it today or tomorrow.

18. She said, (says she) the report is false; and he replied, (says he) if it be not correct I have been misinformed.

19. I took my place in the cars (for) to go to New York.

20. They need not (to) call upon him.

21. Nothing (else) but that would satisfy him.

22. Whenever I ride in the cars I (always) find it prejudicial to my health.

23. He was the first (of all) at the meeting.

24. He was the tallest of (all) the brothers.

25. You are the tallest of (all) your family.

26. Whenever I pass the house he is (always) at the door.

27. The rain has penetrated (through) the roof.

28. Besides my uncle and aunt there was (also) my grandfather.

29. It should (ever) be your constant endeavor to please your family.

30. If it is true as you have heard (then) his situation is indeed pitiful.

31. Either this (here) man or that (there) woman has (got) it.

32. Where is the fire (at)?

33. Did you sleep? Not that I know (of).

34. I never before (in my life) met (with) such a stupid man.

35. (For) why did he postpone it?

36. Because (why) he could not attend.

37. What age is he? (Why) I don't know.

38. He called on me (for) to ask my opinion.

39. I don't know where I am (at).

40.   I looked in (at) the window.

41.   I passed (by) the house.

42.   He (always) came every Sunday.

43.   Moreover, (also) we wish to say he was in error.

44.   It is not long (ago) since he was here.

45.   Two men went into the wood (in order) to cut (down) trees.

Further examples of redundancy might be multiplied. It is very common in newspaper writing where not alone single words but entire phrases are sometimes brought in, which are unnecessary to the sense or explanation of what is written.

GRAMMATICAL ERRORS OF STANDARD AUTHORS

Even the best speakers and writers are sometimes caught napping. Many of our standard authors to whom we have been accustomed to look up as infallible have sinned more or less against the fundamental principles of grammar by breaking the rules regarding one or more of the nine parts of speech. In fact some of them have recklessly trespassed against all nine, and still they sit on their pedestals of fame for the admiration of the crowd. Macaulay mistreated the article. He wrote, —"That *a* historian should not record trifles is perfectly true." He should have used *an*.

Dickens also used the article incorrectly. He refers to "Robinson Crusoe" as "*an* universally popular book," instead of *a* universally popular book.

The relation between nouns and pronouns has always been a stumbling block to speakers and writers. Hallam in his *Literature of Europe* writes, "No one as yet had exhibited the structure of the human kidneys, Vesalius having only examined them in dogs." This means that Vesalius examined human kidneys in dogs. The sentence should have been, "No one had as yet exhibited the kidneys in human beings, Vesalius having examined such organs in dogs only."

Sir Arthur Helps in writing of Dickens, states—"I knew a brother author of his who received such criticisms from him (Dickens) very lately and profited by *it*." Instead of *it* the word should be *them* to agree with criticisms.

Here are a few other pronominal errors from leading authors:

"Sir Thomas Moore in general so writes it, although not many others so late as *him*." Should be *he*. —Trench's *English Past and Present*.

"What should we gain by it but that we should speedily become as poor as *them*." Should be *they*.— Alison's *Essay on Macaulay*.

"If the king gives us leave you or I may as lawfully preach, as *them* that do." Should be *they* or *those*, the latter having persons understood.—Hobbes's *History of Civil Wars*.

"The drift of all his sermons was, to prepare the Jews for the reception of a prophet, mightier than *him*, and whose shoes he was not worthy to bear." Should be than *he*.—Atterbury's *Sermons*.

"Phalaris, who was so much older than *her*." Should be *she*.—Bentley's *Dissertation on Phalaris*.

"King Charles, and more than *him*, the duke and the Popish faction were at liberty to form new schemes." Should be than *he*.—Bolingbroke's *Dissertations on Parties*.

"We contributed a third more than the Dutch, who were obliged to the same proportion more than *us*." Should be than *we*.—Swift's *Conduct of the Allies*.

In all the above examples the objective cases of the pronouns have been used while the construction calls for nominative cases.

"Let *thou* and *I* the battle try"—*Anon*.

Here *let* is the governing verb and requires an objective case after it; therefore instead of *thou* and *I*, the words should be *you* (*sing*.) and *me*.

"Forever in this humble cell, Let thee and I, my fair one, dwell"—*Prior*.

Here *thee* and *I* should be the objectives *you* and *me*.

The use of the relative pronoun trips the greatest number of authors.

Even in the Bible we find the relative wrongly translated:

Whom do men say that I am?—*St. Matthew*.

Whom think ye that I am?—*Acts of the Apostles*.

Who should be written in both cases because the word is not in the objective governed by say or think, but in the nominative dependent on the verb *am*.

"*Who* should I meet at the coffee house t'other night, but my old friend?"—*Steele*.

"It is another pattern of this answerer's fair dealing, to give us hints that the author is dead, and yet lay the suspicion upon somebody, I know not *who*, in the country."—Swift's *Tale of a Tub*.

"My son is going to be married to I don't know *who*." —Goldsmith's *Good-natured Man*.

The nominative *who* in the above examples should be the objective *whom*.

The plural nominative *ye* of the pronoun *thou* is very often used for the objective *you*, as in the following:

"His wrath which will one day destroy *ye both*." —*Milton.*

"The more shame for *ye*; holy men I thought *ye*."—*Shakespeare.*

"I feel the gales that from *ye* blow."—*Gray.*

"Tyrants dread *ye*, lest your just decree Transfer the power and set the people free."—*Prior.*

Many of the great writers have played havoc with the adjective in the indiscriminate use of the degrees of comparison.

"Of two forms of the same word, use the fittest."—*Morell.*

The author here in *trying* to give good advice sets a bad example. He should have used the comparative degree, "Fitter."

Adjectives which have a comparative or superlative signification do not admit the addition of the words *more*, *most*, or the terminations, *er*, *est*, hence the following examples break this rule:

"Money is the *most universal* incitement of human misery."—Gibbon's *Decline and Fall.*

"The *chiefest* of which was known by the name of Archon among the Grecians."—Dryden's *Life of Plutarch.*

"The *chiefest* and largest are removed to certain magazines they call libraries."—Swift's *Battle of the Books.*

The two *chiefest* properties of air, its gravity and elastic force, have been discovered by mechanical experiments.—*Arbuthno*

"From these various causes, which in greater or *lesser* degree, affected every individual in the colony, the indignation of the people became general."—Robertson's *History of America.*

"The *extremest* parts of the earth were meditating a submission."—Atterbury's *Sermons.*

"The last are indeed *more preferable* because they are founded on some new knowledge or improvement in the mind of man."—Addison, *Spectator.*

"This was in reality the *easiest* manner of the two."—Shaftesbury's *Advice to an Author.*

"In every well formed mind this second desire seems to be the *strongest* of the two."—Smith's *Theory of Moral Sentiments.*

In these examples the superlative is wrongly used for the comparative. When only two objects are compared the comparative form must be used.

Of impossibility there are no degrees of comparison, yet we find the following:

"As it was impossible they should know the words, thoughts and secret actions of all men, so it was *more impossible* they should pass judgment on them according to these things."

A great number of authors employ adjectives for adverbs. Thus we find:

"I shall endeavor to live hereafter *suitable* to a man in my station."—*Addison.*

"I can never think so very *mean* of him."—Bentley's *Dissertation on Phalaris.*

"His expectations run high and the fund to supply them is *extreme* scanty,—*Lancaster's Essay on Delicacy.*

The commonest error in the use of the verb is the disregard of the concord between the verb and its subject. This occurs most frequently when the subject and the verb are widely separated, especially if some other noun of a different number immediately precedes the verb. False concords occur very often after *either, or, neither, nor,* and *much, more, many, everyone, each.*

Here are a few authors' slips:—

"The terms in which the sale of a patent *were* communicated to the public."—Junius's *Letters.*

"The richness of her arms and apparel *were* conspicuous."—Gibbon's *Decline and Fall.*

"Everyone of this grotesque family *were* the creatures of national genius."—D'Israeli.

"He knows not what spleen, languor or listlessness *are.*"—Blair's *Sermons.*

"Each of these words *imply*, some pursuit or object relinquished."—*Ibid.*

"Magnus, with four thousand of his supposed accomplices *were* put to death."—*Gibbon.*

"No nation gives greater encouragements to learning than we do; yet at the same time *none are* so injudicious in the application."—*Goldsmith.*

"*There's two* or *three* of us have seen strange sights."—*Shakespeare.*

The past participle should not be used for the past tense, yet the learned Byron overlooked this fact. He thus writes in the *Lament of Tasso:*—

"And with my years my soul *begun to pant* With feelings of strange tumult and soft pain."

Here is another example from Savage's *Wanderer* in which there is double sinning:

"From liberty each nobler science *sprung*, A Bacon brighten'd and a Spenser *sung*."

Other breaches in regard to the participles occur in the following:—

"Every book ought to be read with the same spirit and in the same manner as it is *writ*"—Fielding's *Tom Jones*.

"The Court of Augustus had not *wore* off the manners of the republic "—Hume's *Essays*.

"Moses tells us that the fountains of the earth were *broke* open or clove asunder."—Burnet.

"A free constitution when it has been *shook* by the iniquity of former administrations."—*Bolingbroke*.

"In this respect the seeds of future divisions were *sowed* abundantly."—*Ibid*.

In the following example the present participle is used for the infinitive mood:

"It is easy *distinguishing* the rude fragment of a rock from the splinter of a statue."—Gilfillan's *Literary Portraits*.

Distinguishing here should be replaced by *to distinguish*.

The rules regarding *shall* and *will* are violated in the following:

"If we look within the rough and awkward outside, we *will* be richly rewarded by its perusal."—Gilfillan's *Literary Portraits*.

"If I *should* declare them and speak of them, they should be more than I am able to express."—*Prayer Book Revision of Psalms XI*.

"If I *would* declare them and speak of them, they are more than can be numbered."—*Ibid*.

"Without having attended to this, we *will* be at a loss, in understanding several passages in the classics."—Blair's *Lectures*.

"We know to what cause our past reverses have been owing and *we* will have ourselves to blame, if they are again incurred."—Alison's *History of Europe*.

Adverbial mistakes often occur in the best writers. The adverb *rather* is a word very frequently misplaced. Archbishop Trench in his "English Past and Present" writes, "It *rather* modified the structure of our sentences than the elements of our vocabulary." This should have been written,—"It modified the structure of our sentences *rather than* the elements of our vocabulary."

"So far as his mode of teaching goes he is *rather* a disciple of Socrates than of St. Paul or Wesley." Thus writes Leslie Stephens of Dr. Johnson. He should have written,—" So far as his mode of teaching goes he is a disciple of Socrates *rather* than of St. Paul or Wesley."

The preposition is a part of speech which is often wrongly used by some of the best writers. Certain nouns, adjectives and verbs require particular prepositions after them, for instance, the word *different* always takes the preposition *from* after it; *prevail* takes *upon*; *averse* takes *to*; *accord* takes *with*, and so on.

In the following examples the prepositions in parentheses are the ones that should have been used:

"He found the greatest difficulty *of* (in) writing."—Hume's *History of England*.

"If policy can prevail *upon* (over) force."—*Addison*.

"He made the discovery and communicated *to* (with) his friends."—Swift's *Tale of a Tub*.

"Every office of command should be intrusted to persons *on* (in) whom the parliament shall confide."—*Macaulay*.

Several of the most celebrated writers infringe the canons of style by placing prepositions at the end of sentences. For instance Carlyle, in referring to the Study of Burns, writes:—"Our own contributions to it, we are aware, can be but scanty and feeble; but we offer them with good will, and trust they may meet with acceptance from those they are intended *for*."

—"for whom they are intended," he should have written.

"Most writers have some one vein which they peculiarly and obviously excel *in*."—*William Minto*.

This sentence should read,—Most writers have some one vein in which they peculiarly and obviously excel.

Many authors use redundant words which repeat the same thought and idea. This is called tautology.

"Notwithstanding which (however) poor Polly embraced them all around."—*Dickens*.

"I judged that they would (mutually) find each other."—*Crockett*.

"....as having created a (joint) partnership between the two Powers in the Morocco question."—*The Times*.

"The only sensible position (there seems to be) is to frankly acknowledge our ignorance of what lies beyond."—*Daily Telegraph*.

"Lord Rosebery has not budged from his position—splendid, no doubt,—of (lonely) isolation."—*The Times*.

"Miss Fox was (often) in the habit of assuring Mrs. Chick."—*Dickens*.

"The deck (it) was their field of fame."—*Campbell*.

"He had come up one morning, as was now (frequently) his wont,"—*Trollope*.

The counsellors of the Sultan (continue to) remain sceptical—*The Times*.

Seriously, (and apart from jesting), this is no light matter.—*Bagehot*.

To go back to your own country with (the consciousness that you go back with) the sense of duty well done.—*Lord Halsbury*.

The *Peresviet* lost both her fighting-tops and (in appearance) looked the most damaged of all the ships—*The Times*.

Counsel admitted that, that was a fair suggestion to make, but he submitted that it was borne out by the (surrounding) circumstances.—*Ibid*.

Another unnecessary use of words and phrases is that which is termed circumlocution, a going around the bush when there is no occasion for it,—save to fill space.

It may be likened to a person walking the distance of two sides of a triangle to reach the objective point. For instance in the quotation: "Pope professed to have learned his poetry from Dryden, whom, whenever an opportunity was presented, he praised through the whole period of his existence with unvaried liberality; and perhaps his character may receive some illustration, of a comparison he instituted between him and the man whose pupil he was" much of the verbiage may be eliminated and the sentence thus condensed:

"Pope professed himself the pupil of Dryden, whom he lost no opportunity of praising; and his character may be illustrated by a comparison with his master."

"His life was brought to a close in 1910 at an age not far from the one fixed by the sacred writer as the term of human existence."

This in brevity can be put, "His life was brought to a close at the age of seventy;" or, better yet, "He died at the age of seventy."

"The day was intensely cold, so cold in fact that the thermometer crept down to the zero mark," can be expressed: "The day was so cold the thermometer registered zero."

Many authors resort to circumlocution for the purpose of "padding," that is, filling space, or when they strike a snag in writing upon subjects of which they know little or nothing. The young writer should steer clear of it and learn to express his thoughts and ideas as briefly as possible commensurate with lucidity of expression.

Volumes of errors in fact, in grammar, diction and general style, could be selected from the works of the great writers, a fact which eloquently testifies that no one is infallible and that the very best is liable to err at times. However, most of the erring in the case of these writers arises from carelessness or hurry, not from a lack of knowledge.

As a general rule it is in writing that the scholar is liable to slip; in oral speech he seldom makes a blunder. In fact, there are many people who are perfect masters of speech,—who never make a blunder in conversation, yet who are ignorant of the very principles of grammar and would not know how to write a sentence correctly on paper. Such persons have been accustomed from infancy to hear the language spoken correctly and so the use of the proper words and forms becomes a second nature to them. A child can learn what is right as easy as what is wrong and whatever impressions are made on the mind when it is plastic will remain there. Even a parrot can be taught the proper use of language. Repeat to a parrot.—"Two and two *make* four" and it never will say "two and two *makes* four."

In writing, however, it is different. Without a knowledge of the fundamentals of grammar we may be able to speak correctly from association with good speakers, but without such a knowledge we cannot hope to write the language correctly. To write even a common letter we must know the principles of construction, the relationship of one word to another. Therefore, it is necessary for everybody to understand at least the essentials of the grammar of his own language.

CHAPTER VIII

PITFALLS TO AVOID

Common Stumbling Blocks—Peculiar Constructions—Misused Forms.

ATTRACTION

Very often the verb is separated from its real nominative or subject by several intervening words and in such cases one is liable to make the verb agree with the subject nearest to it. Here are a few examples showing that the leading writers now and then take a tumble into this pitfall:

1. "The partition which the two ministers made of the powers of government *were* singularly happy."—*Macaulay*.

   (Should be *was* to agree with its subject, *partition*.)

2. "One at least of the qualities which fit it for training ordinary men *unfit* it for *training* an extraordinary man."—*Bagehot*.

   (Should be *unfits* to agree with subject *one*.)

3. "The Tibetans have engaged to exclude from their country those dangerous influences whose appearance *were* the chief cause of our action."—*The Times*.

   (Should be *was* to agree with *appearance*.)

4. "An immense amount of confusion and indifference *prevail* in these days."—*Telegraph*.

   (Should be *prevails* to agree with amount.)

ELLIPSIS

Errors in ellipsis occur chiefly with prepositions.

His objection and condoning of the boy's course, seemed to say the least, paradoxical.

(The preposition *to* should come after objection.)

Many men of brilliant parts are crushed by force of circumstances and their genius forever lost to the world.

(Some maintain that the missing verb after genius is *are*, but such is ungrammatical. In such cases the right verb should be always expressed: as—their genius *is* forever lost to the world.

THE SPLIT INFINITIVE

Even the best speakers and writers are in the habit of placing a modifying word or words between the *to* and the remaining part of the infinitive. It is possible that such will come to be looked upon in time as the proper form but at present the splitting of the infinitive is decidedly wrong. "He was scarcely able *to* even *talk*" "She commenced *to* rapidly *walk* around the room." "*To have* really *loved* is better than not *to have* at all *loved*." In these constructions it is much better not to split the infinitive. In every-day speech the best speakers sin against this observance.

In New York City there is a certain magistrate, a member of "the 400," who prides himself on his diction in language. He tells this story: A prisoner, a faded, battered specimen of mankind, on whose haggard face, deeply lined with the marks of dissipation, there still lingered faint reminders of better days long past, stood dejected before the judge. "Where are you from?" asked the magistrate. "From Boston," answered the accused. "Indeed," said the judge, "indeed, yours is a sad case, and yet you don't seem *to* thoroughly *realise* how low you have sunk." The man stared as if struck. "Your honor does me an injustice," he said bitterly. "The disgrace of arrest for drunkenness, the mortification of being thrust into a noisome dungeon, the publicity and humiliation of trial in a crowded and dingy courtroom I can bear, but to be sentenced by a Police Magistrate who *splits his infinitives*—that is indeed the last blow."

ONE

The indefinite adjective pronoun *one* when put in place of a personal substantive is liable to raise confusion. When a sentence or expression is begun with the impersonal *one* the word must be used throughout in all references to the subject. Thus, "One must mind one's own business if one wishes to succeed" may seem prolix and awkward, nevertheless it is the proper form. You must not say —"One must mind his business if he wishes to succeed," for the subject is impersonal and therefore cannot exclusively take the masculine pronoun. With *any one* it is different. You may say—"If any one sins he should acknowledge it; let him not try to hide it by another sin."

ONLY

This is a word that is a pitfall to the most of us whether learned or unlearned. Probably it is the most indiscriminately used word in the language. From the different positions it is made to occupy in a sentence it can relatively change the meaning. For instance in the sentence—"I *only* struck him that time," the meaning to be inferred is, that the only thing I did to him was to *strike* him, not kick or otherwise abuse him. But if the *only* is shifted, so as to make the sentence read-"I struck him *only* that time" the meaning conveyed is, that only on that occasion and at no other time did I strike him. If another shift is made to-"I struck *only* him that time," the meaning is again altered so that it signifies he was the only person I struck.

In speaking we can by emphasis impress our meaning on our hearers, but in writing we have nothing to depend upon but the position of the word in the sentence. The best rule in regard to *only* is to place it *immediately before* the word or phrase it modifies or limits.

122

ALONE

is another word which creates ambiguity and alters meaning. If we substitute it for only in the preceding example the meaning of the sentence will depend upon the arrangement. Thus "I *alone* struck him at that time" signifies that I and no other struck him. When the sentence reads "I struck him *alone* at that time" it must be interpreted that he was the only person that received a blow. Again if it is made to read "I struck him at that time *alone*" the sense conveyed is that that was the only occasion on which I struck him. The rule which governs the correct use of *only* is also applicable to *alone*.

OTHER AND ANOTHER

These are words which often give to expressions a meaning far from that intended. Thus, "I have *nothing* to do with that *other* rascal across the street," certainly means that I am a rascal myself. "I sent the despatch to my friend, but another villain intercepted it," clearly signifies that my friend is a villain.

A good plan is to omit these words when they can be readily done without, as in the above examples, but when it is necessary to use them make your meaning clear. You can do this by making each sentence or phrase in which they occur independent of contextual aid.

AND WITH THE RELATIVE

Never use *and* with the *relative* in this manner: "That is the dog I meant *and which* I know is of pure breed." This is an error quite common. The use of *and* is permissible when there is a parallel relative in the preceding sentence or clause. Thus: "There is the dog which I meant and.which I know is of pure breed" is quite correct.

LOOSE PARTICIPLES

A participle or participial phrase is naturally referred to the nearest nominative. If only one nominative is expressed it claims all the participles that are not by the construction of the sentence otherwise fixed. "John, working in the field all day and getting thirsty, drank from the running stream." Here the participles *working* and *getting* clearly refer to John. But in the sentence, —"Swept along by the mob I could not save him," the participle as it were is lying around loose and may be taken to refer to either the person speaking or to the person spoken about. It may mean that I was swept along by the mob or the individual whom I tried to save was swept along.

"Going into the store the roof fell" can be taken that it was the roof which was going into the store when it fell. Of course the meaning intended is that some person or persons were going into the store just as the roof fell.

In all sentence construction with participles there should be such clearness as to preclude all possibility of ambiguity. The participle should be so placed that there can be no doubt as to the noun to which it refers. Often it is advisable to supply such words as will make the meaning obvious.

BROKEN CONSTRUCTION

Sometimes the beginning of a sentence presents quite a different grammatical construction from its end. This arises from the fact probably, that the beginning is lost sight of before the end is reached. This occurs frequently in long sentences. Thus: "Honesty, integrity and square-dealing will bring anybody much better through life than the absence of either." Here the construction is broken at *than*. The use of *either*, only used in referring to one of two, shows that the fact is forgotten that three qualities and not two are under consideration. Any one of the three meanings might be intended in the sentence, viz., absence of any one quality, absence of any two of the qualities or absence of the whole three qualities. Either denotes one or the other of two and should never be applied to any one of more than two. When we fall into the error of constructing such sentences as above, we should take them apart and reconstruct them in a different grammatical form. Thus, —"Honesty, integrity and square-dealing will bring a man much better through life than a lack of these qualities which are almost essential to success."

DOUBLE NEGATIVE

It must be remembered that two negatives in the English language destroy each other and are equivalent to an affirmative. Thus "I *don't* know *nothing* about it" is intended to convey, that I am ignorant of the matter under consideration, but it defeats its own purpose, inasmuch as the use of nothing implies that I know something about it. The sentence should read—"I don't know anything about it."

Often we hear such expressions as "He was *not* asked to give *no* opinion," expressing the very opposite of what is intended. This sentence implies that he was asked to give his opinion. The double negative, therefore, should be carefully avoided, for it is insidious and is liable to slip in and the writer remain unconscious of its presence until the eye of the critic detects it.

FIRST PERSONAL PRONOUN

The use of the first personal pronoun should be avoided as much as possible in composition. Don't introduce it by way of apology and never use such expressions as "In my opinion," "As far as I can see," "It appears to me," "I believe," etc. In what you write, the whole composition is expressive of your views, since you are the author, therefore, there is no necessity for you to accentuate or emphasize yourself at certain portions of it.

Moreover, the big *I's* savor of egotism! Steer clear of them as far as you can. The only place where the first person is permissible is in passages where you are stating a view that is not generally held and which is likely to meet with opposition.

SEQUENCE OF TENSES

When two verbs depend on each other their tenses must have a definite relation to each other. "I shall have much pleasure in accepting your kind invitation" is wrong, unless you really mean that just now you decline though by-and-by you intend to accept; or unless you mean that you do accept now, though you have no pleasure in doing so, but look forward to be more pleased by-and-by. In fact the sequence of the compound tenses puzzle experienced writers. The best plan is to go back in thought to the time in question and use the tense you would *then* naturally use. Now in the sentence "I should have liked to have gone to see the circus" the way to find out the proper sequence is to ask yourself the question—what is it I "should have liked" to do? and the plain answer is "to go to see the circus." I cannot answer—"To have gone to see the circus" for that would imply that at a certain moment I would have liked to be in the position of having gone to the circus. But I do not mean this; I mean that at the moment at which I am speaking I wish I had gone to see the circus. The verbal phrase *I should have liked* carries me back to the time when there was a chance of seeing the circus and once back at the time, the going to the circus is a thing of the present. This whole explanation resolves itself into the simple question,—what should I have liked *at that time*, and the answer is "to go to see the circus," therefore this is the proper sequence, and the expression should be "I should have liked to go to see the circus."

If we wish to speak of something relating to a time *prior* to that indicated in the past tense we must use the perfect tense of the infinitive; as, "He appeared to have seen better days." We should say "I expected to *meet him*," not "I expected *to have met him*." "We intended *to visit you*," not "*to have visited* you." "I hoped they *would* arrive," not "I hoped they *would have* arrived." "I thought I should *catch* the bird," not "I thought I should *have caught* the bird." "I had intended *to go* to the meeting," not "I had intended *to have gone* to the meeting."

BETWEEN—AMONG

These prepositions are often carelessly interchanged. *Between* has reference to two objects only, *among* to more than two. "The money was equally divided between them" is right when there are only two, but if there are more than two it should be "the money was equally divided among them."

LESS—FEWER

Less refers is quantity, *fewer* to number. "No man has *less* virtues" should be "No man has *fewer* virtues." "The farmer had some oats and a *fewer* quantity of wheat" should be "the farmer had some oats and a *less* quantity of wheat."

FURTHER—FARTHER

Further is commonly used to denote quantity, *farther* to denote distance. "I have walked *farther* than you," "I need no *further* supply" are correct.

EACH OTHER—ONE ANOTHER

Each other refers to two, *one another* to more than two. "Jones and Smith quarreled; they struck each other" is correct. "Jones, Smith and Brown quarreled; they struck one another" is also correct. Don't say, "The two boys teach one another" nor "The three girls love each other."

EACH, EVERY, EITHER, NEITHER

These words are continually misapplied. *Each* can be applied to two or any higher number of objects to signify *every one* of the number *independently*. Every requires *more than two* to be spoken of and denotes all the *persons* or *things* taken *separately. Either* denotes *one or the other of two*, and should not be used to include both. *Neither* is the negative of either, denoting not the other, and not the one, and relating to *two persons* or *things* considered separately.

The following examples illustrate the correct usage of these words:

Each man of the crew received a reward.

Every man in the regiment displayed bravery.

We can walk on *either* side of the street.

Neither of the two is to blame.

NEITHER-NOR

When two singular subjects are connected by *neither, nor* use a singular verb; as, *Neither* John *nor* James *was there*," not *were* there.

NONE

Custom Has sanctioned the use of this word both with a singular and plural; as—"None *is* so blind as he who will not see" and "None *are* so blind as they who will not see." However, as it is a contraction of *no one* it is better to use the singular verb.

RISE-RAISE

These verbs are very often confounded. *Rise* is to move or pass upward in any manner; as to "rise from bed;" to increase in value, to improve in position or rank, as "stocks rise;" "politicians rise;" "they have risen to honor."

Raise is to lift up, to exalt, to enhance, as "I raise the table;" "He raised his servant;" "The baker raised the price of *bread*."

LAY-LIE

The transitive verb *lay*, and *lay*, the past tense of the neuter verb *lie*, are often confounded, though quite different in meaning. The neuter verb *to lie*, meaning to lie down or rest, cannot take the objective after it except with a preposition. We can say "He *lies* on the ground," but we cannot say "He *lies* the ground," since the verb is neuter and intransitive and, as such, cannot have a direct object. With *lay* it is different. *Lay* is a transitive verb, therefore it takes a direct object after it; as "I *lay* a wager," "I *laid* the carpet," etc.

Of a carpet or any inanimate subject we should say, "It lies on the floor," "A knife *lies* on the table," not *lays*. But of a person we say—"He *lays* the knife on the table," not "He *lies*———." *Lay* being the

126

past tense of the neuter to lie (down) we should say, "He *lay* on the bed," and *lain* being its past participle we must also say "He has *lain* on the bed."

We can say "I lay myself down." "He laid himself down" and such expressions.

It is imperative to remember in using these verbs that to *lay* means *to do* something, and to lie means *to be in a state of rest.*

SAYS I—I SAID

"Says I" is a vulgarism; don't use it. "I said" is correct form.

IN—INTO

Be careful to distinguish the meaning of these two little prepositions and don't interchange them. Don't say "He went *in* the room" nor "My brother is *into* the navy." *In* denotes the place where a person or thing, whether at rest or in motion, is present; and *into* denotes *entrance.* "He went *into* the room;" "My brother is *in* the navy" are correct.

EAT—ATE

Don't confound the two. *Eat* is present, *ate* is past. "I *eat* the bread" means that I am continuing the eating; "I *ate* the bread" means that the act of eating is past. *Eaten* is the perfect participle, but often *eat* is used instead, and as it has the same pronunciation (et) of *ate*, care should be taken to distinguish the past tense, I *ate* from the perfect *I have eaten (eat).*

SEQUENCE OF PERSON

Remember that the *first* person takes precedence of the *second* and the *second* takes precedence of the *third.* When Cardinal Wolsey said *Ego et Rex* (I and the King), he showed he was a good grammarian, but a bad courtier.

AM COME—HAVE COME

"I am come" points to my being here, while "I have come" intimates that I have just arrived. When the subject is not a person, the verb *to be* should be used in preference to the verb *to have*; as, "The box is come" instead of "The box has come."

PAST TENSE—PAST PARTICIPLE

The interchange of these two parts of the irregular or so-called *strong* verbs is, perhaps, the breach oftenest committed by careless speakers and writers. To avoid mistakes it is requisite to know the principal parts of these verbs, and this knowledge is very easy of acquirement, as there are not more than a couple of hundred of such verbs, and of this number but a small part is in daily use. Here are some of the most common blunders: "I seen" for "I saw;" "I done it" for "I did it;" "I drunk" for "I drank;" "I begun" for "I began;" "I rung" for "I rang;" "I run" for "I ran;" "I sung" for "I sang;" "I have chose" for "I have chosen;" "I have drove" for "I have driven;" "I have wore" for "I have worn;" "I have trod" for "I have trodden;" "I have shook" for "I have shaken;" "I have fell" for "I have fallen;" "I have drank" for "I have drunk;" "I have began" for "I have begun;" "I have rang" for "I have rung;" "I have rose" for "I have risen;" "I have spoke" for "I have spoken;" "I have broke" for "I have broken." "It has froze" for "It has frozen." "It has blowed" for "It has blown." "It has flowed" (of a bird) for "It has flown."

N. B.—The past tense and past participle of *To Hang* is *hanged* or *hung*. When you are talking about a man meeting death on the gallows, say "He was hanged"; when you are talking about the carcass of an animal say, "It was hung," as "The beef was hung dry." Also say your coat "*was* hung on a hook."

PREPOSITIONS AND THE OBJECTIVE CASE

Don't forget that prepositions always take the objective case. Don't say "Between you and *I*"; say "Between you and *me*"

Two prepositions should not govern *one objective* unless there is an immediate connection between them. "He was refused admission to and forcibly ejected from the school" should be "He was refused admission to the school and forcibly ejected from it."

SUMMON—SUMMONS

Don't say "I shall summons him," but "I shall summon him." *Summon* is a verb, *summons*, a noun.

It is correct to say "I shall get a *summons* for him," not a *summon*.

UNDENIABLE—UNEXCEPTIONABLE

"My brother has an undeniable character" is wrong if I wish to convey the idea that he has a good character. The expression should be in that case "My brother has an unexceptionable character." An *undeniable* character is a character that cannot be denied, whether bad or good. An unexceptionable character is one to which no one can take exception.

THE PRONOUNS

Very many mistakes occur in the use of the pronouns. "Let you and I go" should be "Let you and *me* go." "Let them and we go" should be "Let them and us go." The verb let is transitive and therefore takes the objective case.

"Give me *them* flowers" should be "Give me *those* flowers"; "I mean *them* three" should be "I mean those three." Them is the objective case of the personal pronoun and cannot be used adjectively like the demonstrative adjective pronoun. "I am as strong as *him*" should be "I am as strong as *he*"; "I am younger than *her*" should be "I am younger than *she*;" "He can write better than *me*" should be "He can write better than I," for in these examples the objective cases *him, her* and *me* are used wrongfully for the nominatives. After each of the misapplied pronouns a verb is understood of

128

which each pronoun is the subject. Thus, "I am as strong as he (is)." "I am younger than she (is)." "He can write better than I (can)."

Don't say "*It is me*;" say "*It is I*" The verb *To Be* of which is is a part takes the same case after it that it has before it. This holds good in all situations as well as with pronouns.

The verb *To Be* also requires the pronouns joined to it to be in the same case as a pronoun asking a question; The nominative *I* requires the nominative *who* and the objectives *me, him, her, its, you, them,* require the objective *whom.*

"*Whom* do you think I am?" should be "*Who* do you think I am?" and "*Who* do they suppose me to be?" should be "*Whom* do they suppose me to be?" The objective form of the Relative should be always used, in connection with a preposition. "Who do you take me for?" should be "*Whom* do, etc." "Who did you give the apple to?" should be "Whom did you give the apple to," but as pointed out elsewhere the preposition should never end a sentence, therefore, it is better to say, "To whom did you give the apple?"

After transitive verbs always use the objective cases of the pronouns. For "*He* and *they* we have seen," say "*Him* and *them* we have seen."

THAT FOR SO

"The hurt it was that painful it made him cry," say "so painful."

THESE—THOSE

Don't say, *These kind; those sort. Kind* and *sort* are each singular and require the singular pronouns *this* and *that.* In connection with these demonstrative adjective pronouns remember that *this* and *these* refer to what is near at hand, *that* and *those* to what is more distant; as, *this book* (near me), *that book* (over there), *these* boys (near), *those* boys (at a distance).

THIS MUCH—THUS MUCH

"*This* much is certain" should be "*Thus* much or *so* much is certain."

FLEE—FLY

These are two separate verbs and must not be interchanged. The principal parts of *flee* are *flee, fled, fled;* those of *fly* are *fly, flew, flown. To flee* is generally used in the meaning of getting out of danger. *To fly* means to soar as a bird. To say of a man "He *has flown* from the place" is wrong; it should be "He *has fled* from the place." We can say with propriety that "A bird has *flown* from the place."

THROUGH—THROUGHOUT

Don't say "He is well known through the land," but "He is well known throughout the land."

VOCATION AND AVOCATION

Don't mistake these two words so nearly alike. Vocation is the employment, business or profession one follows for a living; avocation is some pursuit or occupation which diverts the person from such employment, business or profession. Thus

"His vocation was the law, his avocation, farming."

WAS—WERE

In the subjunctive mood the plural form *were* should be used with a singular subject; as, "If I *were*," not *was*. Remember the plural form of the personal pronoun *you* always takes *were*, though it may denote but one. Thus, "*You were*," never "*you was*." "*If I was him*" is a very common expression. Note the two mistakes in it,—that of the verb implying a condition, and that of the objective case of the pronoun. It should read *If I were he*. This is another illustration of the rule regarding the verb *To Be*, taking the same case after it as before it; *were* is part of the verb *To Be*, therefore as the nominative (I) goes before it, the nominative (he) should come after it.

A OR AN

A becomes an before a vowel or before *h* mute for the sake of euphony or agreeable sound to the ear. *An apple*, *an orange*, *an heir*, *an honor*, etc.

CHAPTER IX

STYLE

Diction—Purity—Propriety—Precision.

It is the object of every writer to put his thoughts into as effective form as possible so as to make a good impression on the reader. A person may have noble thoughts and ideas but be unable to express them in such a way as to appeal to others, consequently he cannot exert the full force of his intellectuality nor leave the imprint of his character upon his time, whereas many a man but indifferently gifted may wield such a facile pen as to attract attention and win for himself an envious place among his contemporaries.

In everyday life one sees illustrations of men of excellent mentality being cast aside and ones of mediocre or in some cases, little, if any, ability chosen to fill important places. The former are unable to impress their personality; they have great thoughts, great ideas, but these thoughts and ideas are locked up in their brains and are like prisoners behind the bars struggling to get free. The key of language which would open the door is wanting, hence they have to remain locked up.

Many a man has to pass through the world unheard of and of little benefit to it or himself, simply because he cannot bring out what is in him and make it subservient to his will. It is the duty of every one to develop his best, not only for the benefit of himself but for the good of his fellow men. It is not at all necessary to have great learning or acquirements, the laborer is as useful in his own place as the philosopher in his; nor is it necessary to have many talents. One talent rightly used is much better than ten wrongly used. Often a man can do more with one than his contemporary can do with ten, often a man can make one dollar go farther than twenty in the hands of his neighbor, often the poor man lives more comfortably than the millionaire. All depends upon the individual himself. If he make right use of what the Creator has given him and live according to the laws of God and nature he is fulfilling his allotted place in the universal scheme of creation, in other words, when he does his best, he is living up to the standard of a useful manhood.

Now in order to do his best a man of ordinary intelligence and education should be able to express himself correctly both in speaking and writing, that is, he should be able to convey his thoughts in an intelligent manner which the simplest can understand. The manner in which a speaker or writer conveys his thoughts is known as his Style. In other words *Style* may be defined as the peculiar manner in which a man expresses his conceptions through the medium of language. It depends upon the choice of words and their arrangement to convey a meaning. Scarcely any two writers have exactly the same style, that is to say, express their ideas after the same peculiar form, just as no two mortals are fashioned by nature in the same mould, so that one is an exact counterpart of the other.

Just as men differ in the accent and tones of their voices, so do they differ in the construction of their language.

Two reporters sent out on the same mission, say to report a fire, will verbally differ in their accounts though materially both descriptions will be the same as far as the leading facts are concerned. One will express himself in a style *different* from the other.

131

If you are asked to describe the dancing of a red-haired lady at the last charity ball you can either say—"The ruby Circe, with the Titian locks glowing like the oriflamme which surrounds the golden god of day as he sinks to rest amid the crimson glory of the burnished West, gave a divine exhibition of the Terpsichorean art which thrilled the souls of the multitude" or, you can simply say —"The red-haired lady danced very well and pleased the audience."

The former is a specimen of the ultra florid or bombastic style which may be said to depend upon the pomposity of verbosity for its effect, the latter is a specimen of simple *natural* Style. Needless to say it is to be preferred. The other should be avoided. It stamps the writer as a person of shallowness, ignorance and inexperience. It has been eliminated from the newspapers. Even the most flatulent of yellow sheets no longer tolerate it in their columns. Affectation and pedantry in style are now universally condemned.

It is the duty of every speaker and writer to labor after a pleasing style. It gains him an entrance where he would otherwise be debarred. Often the interest of a subject depends as much on the way it is presented as on the subject itself. One writer will make it attractive, another repulsive. For instance take a passage in history. Treated by one historian it is like a desiccated mummy, dry, dull, disgusting, while under the spell of another it is, as it were, galvanized into a virile living thing which not only pleases but captivates the reader.

DICTION

The first requisite of style is *choice* of *words,* and this comes under the head of *Diction,* the property of style which has reference to the words and phrases used in speaking and writing. The secret of literary skill from any standpoint consists in putting the right word in the right place. In order to do this it is imperative to know the meaning of the words we use, their exact literal meaning. Many synonymous words are seemingly interchangeable and appear as if the same meaning were applicable to three or four of them at the same time, but when all such words are reduced to a final analysis it is clearly seen that there is a marked difference in their meaning. For instance *grief* and *sorrow* seem to be identical, but they are not. *Grief* is active, *sorrow* is more or less passive; *grief* is caused by troubles and misfortunes which come to us from the outside, while *sorrow* is often the consequence of our own acts. *Grief* is frequently loud and violent, *sorrow* is always quiet and retiring. *Grief* shouts, *Sorrow* remains calm.

If you are not sure of the exact meaning of a word look it up immediately in the dictionary. Sometimes some of our great scholars are puzzled over simple words in regard to meaning, spelling or pronunciation. Whenever you meet a strange word note it down until you discover its meaning and use. Read the best books you can get, books written by men and women who are acknowledged masters of language, and study how they use their words, where they place them in the sentences, and the meanings they convey to the readers.

Mix in good society. Listen attentively to good talkers and try to imitate their manner of expression. If a word is used you do not understand, don't be ashamed to ask its meaning.

True, a small vocabulary will carry you through, but it is an advantage to have a large one. When you live alone a little pot serves just as well as a large one to cook your victuals and it is handy and convenient, but when your friends or neighbors come to dine with you, you will need a much larger pot and it is better to have it in store, so that you will not be put to shame for your scantiness of furnishings.

Get as many words as you possibly can—if you don't need them now, pack them away in the garrets of your brain so that you can call upon them if you require them.

Keep a note book, jot down the words you don't understand or clearly understand and consult the dictionary when you get time.

PURITY

Purity of style consists in using words which are reputable, national and present, which means that the words are in current use by the best authorities, that they are used throughout the nation and not confined to one particular part, and that they are words in constant use at the present time.

There are two guiding principles in the choice of words,—*good use* and *good taste*. *Good use* tells us whether a word is right or wrong; *good taste,* whether it is adapted to our purpose or not.

A word that is obsolete or too new to have gained a place in the language, or that is a provincialism, should not be used.

Here are the Ten Commandments of English style:

1.   Do not use foreign words.

2.   Do not use a long word when a short one will serve your purpose. *Fire* is much better than *conflagration.*

3.   Do not use technical words, or those understood only by specialists in their respective lines, except when you are writing especially for such people.

4.   Do not use slang.

5.   Do not use provincialisms, as "I guess" for "I think"; "I reckon" for "I know," etc.

6.   Do not in writing prose, use poetical or antiquated words: as "lore, e'er, morn, yea, nay, verily, peradventure."

7.   Do not use trite and hackneyed words and expressions; as, "on the job," "up and in"; "down and out."

8.   Do not use newspaper words which have not established a place in the language as "to bugle"; "to suicide," etc.

9.   Do not use ungrammatical words and forms; as, "I ain't;" "he don't."

10.   Do not use ambiguous words or phrases; as—"He showed me all about the house."

Trite words, similes and metaphors which have become hackneyed and worn out should be allowed to rest in the oblivion of past usage. Such expressions and phrases as "Sweet sixteen" "the Almighty dollar," "Uncle Sam," "On the fence," "The Glorious Fourth," "Young America," "The lords of creation," "The rising generation," "The weaker sex," "The weaker vessel," "Sweetness long drawn out" and "chief cook and bottle washer," should be put on the shelf as they are utterly worn out from too much usage.

Some of the old similes which have outlived their usefulness and should be pensioned off, are "Sweet as sugar," "Bold as a lion," "Strong as an ox," "Quick as a flash," "Cold as ice," "Stiff as a poker," "White as snow," "Busy as a bee," "Pale as a ghost," "Rich as Croesus," "Cross as a bear" and a great many more far too numerous to mention.

Be as original as possible in the use of expression. Don't follow in the old rut but try and strike out for yourself. This does not mean that you should try to set the style, or do anything outlandish or out of the way, or be an innovator on the prevailing custom. In order to be original there is no necessity for you to introduce something novel or establish a precedent. The probability is you are not fit to do either, by education or talent. While following the style of those who are acknowledged leaders you can be original in your language. Try and clothe an idea different from what it has been clothed and better. If you are speaking or writing of dancing don't talk or write about "tripping the light fantastic toe." It is over two hundred years since Milton expressed it that way in "*L'Allegro*." You're not a Milton and besides over a million have stolen it from Milton until it is now no longer worth stealing.

Don't resurrect obsolete words such as *whilom, yclept, wis,* etc., and be careful in regard to obsolescent words, that is, words that are at the present time gradually passing from use such as *quoth, trow, betwixt, amongst, froward,* etc.

And beware of new words. Be original in the construction and arrangement of your language, but don't try to originate words. Leave that to the Masters of language, and don't be the first to try such words, wait until the chemists of speech have tested them and passed upon their merits.

Quintilian said—"Prefer the oldest of the new and the newest of the old." Pope put this in rhyme and it still holds good:

In words, as fashions, the same rule will hold, Alike fantastic, if too new or old: Be not the first by whom the new are tried, Nor yet the last to lay the old aside.

PROPRIETY

Propriety of style consists in using words in their proper sense and as in the case of purity, good usage is the principal test. Many words have acquired in actual use a meaning very different from what they once possessed. "Prevent" formerly meant to go before, and that meaning is implied in its Latin derivation. Now it means to put a stop to, to hinder. To attain propriety of style it is necessary to avoid confounding words derived from the same root; as *respectfully* and *respectively*; it is necessary to use words in their accepted sense or the sense which everyday use sanctions.

SIMPLICITY

Simplicity of style has reference to the choice of simple words and their unaffected presentation. Simple words should always be used in preference to compound, and complicated ones when they express the same or almost the same meaning. The Anglo-Saxon element in our language comprises the simple words which express the relations of everyday life, strong, terse, vigorous, the language of the fireside, street, market and farm. It is this style which characterizes the Bible and many of the great English classics such as the "Pilgrim's Progress," "Robinson Crusoe," and "Gulliver's Travels."

CLEARNESS

Clearness of style should be one of the leading considerations with the beginner in composition. He must avoid all obscurity and ambiguous phrases. If he write a sentence or phrase and see that a meaning might be inferred from it otherwise than intended, he should re-write it in such a way that there can be no possible doubt. Words, phrases or clauses that are closely related should be placed as near to each other as possible that their mutual relation may clearly appear, and no word should be omitted that is necessary to the complete expression of thought.

UNITY

Unity is that property of style which keeps all parts of a sentence in connection with the principal thought and logically subordinate to it. A sentence may be constructed as to suggest the idea of oneness to the mind, or it may be so loosely put together as to produce a confused and indefinite impression. Ideas that have but little connection should be expressed in separate sentences, and not crowded into one.

Keep long parentheses out of the middle of your sentences and when you have apparently brought your sentences to a close don't try to continue the thought or idea by adding supplementary clauses.

STRENGTH

Strength is that property of style which gives animation, energy and vivacity to language and sustains the interest of the reader. It is as necessary to language as good food is to the body. Without it the words are weak and feeble and create little or no impression on the mind. In order to have strength the language must be concise, that is, much expressed in little compass, you must hit the nail fairly on the head and drive it in straight. Go critically over what you write and strike out every word, phrase and clause the omission of which impairs neither the clearness nor force of the sentence and so avoid redundancy, tautology and circumlocution. Give the most important words the most prominent places, which, as has been pointed out elsewhere, are the beginning and end of the sentence.

HARMONY

Harmony is that property of style which gives a smoothness to the sentence, so that when the words are sounded their connection becomes pleasing to the ear. It adapts sound to sense. Most people construct their sentences without giving thought to the way they will sound and as a consequence we have many jarring and discordant combinations such as "Thou strengthenedst thy position and actedst arbitrarily and derogatorily to my interests."

Harsh, disagreeable verbs are liable to occur with the Quaker form *Thou* of the personal pronoun. This form is now nearly obsolete, the plural *you* being almost universally used. To obtain harmony in the sentence long words that are hard to pronounce and combinations of letters of one kind should be avoided.

EXPRESSIVE OF WRITER

Style is expressive of the writer, as to who he is and what he is. As a matter of structure in composition it is the indication of what a man can do; as a matter of quality it is an indication of what he is.

KINDS OF STYLE

Style has been classified in different ways, but it admits of so many designations that it is very hard to enumerate a table. In fact there are as many styles as there are writers, for no two authors write *exactly* after the same form. However, we may classify the styles of the various authors in broad divisions as (1) dry, (2) plain, (3) neat, (4) elegant, (5) florid, (6) bombastic.

The *dry* style excludes all ornament and makes no effort to appeal to any sense of beauty. Its object is simply to express the thoughts in a correct manner. This style is exemplified by Berkeley.

The *plain* style does not seek ornamentation either, but aims to make clear and concise statements without any elaboration or embellishment. Locke and Whately illustrate the plain style.

The *neat* style only aspires after ornament sparingly. Its object is to have correct figures, pure diction and clear and harmonious sentences. Goldsmith and Gray are the acknowledged leaders in this kind of style.

The *elegant* style uses every ornament that can beautify and avoids every excess which would degrade. Macaulay and Addison have been enthroned as the kings of this style. To them all writers bend the knee in homage.

The *florid* style goes to excess in superfluous and superficial ornamentation and strains after a highly colored imagery. The poems of Ossian typify this style.

The *bombastic* is characterized by such an excess of words, figures and ornaments as to be ridiculous and disgusting. It is like a circus clown dressed up in gold tinsel Dickens gives a fine example of it in Sergeant Buzfuz' speech in the "Pickwick Papers." Among other varieties of style may be mentioned the colloquial, the laconic, the concise, the diffuse, the abrupt the flowing, the quaint, the epigrammatic, the flowery, the feeble, the nervous, the vehement, and the affected. The manner of these is sufficiently indicated by the adjective used to describe them.

In fact style is as various as character and expresses the individuality of the writer, or in other words, as the French writer Buffon very aptly remarks, "the style is the man himself."

CHAPTER X

SUGGESTIONS

How to Write—What to Write—Correct Speaking and Speakers

Rules of grammar and rhetoric are good in their own place; their laws must be observed in order to express thoughts and ideas in the right way so that they shall convey a determinate sense and meaning in a pleasing and acceptable manner. Hard and fast rules, however, can never make a writer or author. That is the business of old Mother Nature and nothing can take her place. If nature has not endowed a man with faculties to put his ideas into proper composition he cannot do so. He may have no ideas worthy the recording. If a person has not a thought to express, it cannot be expressed. Something cannot be manufactured out of nothing. The author must have thoughts and ideas before he can express them on paper. These come to him by nature and environment and are developed and strengthened by study. There is an old Latin quotation in regard to the poet which says "Poeta nascitur non fit" the translation of which is—the poet is born, not made. To a great degree the same applies to the author. Some men are great scholars as far as book learning is concerned, yet they cannot express themselves in passable composition. Their knowledge is like gold locked up in a chest where it is of no value to themselves or the rest of the world.

The best way to learn to write is to sit down and write, just as the best way how to learn to ride a bicycle is to mount the wheel and pedal away. Write first about common things, subjects that are familiar to you. Try for instance an essay on a cat. Say something original about her. Don't say "she is very playful when young but becomes grave as she grows old." That has been said more than fifty thousand times before. Tell what you have seen the family cat doing, how she caught a mouse in the garret and what she did after catching it. Familiar themes are always the best for the beginner. Don't attempt to describe a scene in Australia if you have never been there and know nothing of the country. Never hunt for subjects, there are thousands around you. Describe what you saw yesterday —a fire, a runaway horse, a dog-fight on the street and be original in your description. Imitate the best writers in their *style*, but not in their exact words. Get out of the beaten path, make a pathway of your own.

Know what you write about, write about what you know; this is a golden rule to which you must adhere. To know you must study. The world is an open book in which all who run may read. Nature is one great volume the pages of which are open to the peasant as well as to the peer. Study Nature's moods and tenses, for they are vastly more important than those of the grammar. Book learning is most desirable, but, after all, it is only theory and not practice. The grandest allegory in the English, in fact, in any language, was written by an ignorant, so-called ignorant, tinker named John Bunyan. Shakespeare was not a scholar in the sense we regard the term to-day, yet no man ever lived or probably ever will live that equalled or will equal him in the expression of thought. He simply read the book of nature and interpreted it from the standpoint of his own magnificent genius.

Don't imagine that a college education is necessary to success as a writer. Far from it. Some of our college men are dead-heads, drones, parasites on the body social, not alone useless to the world but to themselves. A person may be so ornamental that he is valueless from any other standpoint. As a general rule ornamental things serve but little purpose. A man may know so much of everything that he knows little of anything. This may sound paradoxical, but, nevertheless, experience proves its truth.

If you are poor that is not a detriment but an advantage. Poverty is an incentive to endeavor, not a drawback. Better to be born with a good, working brain in your head than with a gold spoon in your mouth. If the world had been depending on the so-called pets of fortune it would have deteriorated long ago.

From the pits of poverty, from the arenas of suffering, from the hovels of neglect, from the backwood cabins of obscurity, from the lanes and by-ways of oppression, from the dingy garrets and basements of unending toil and drudgery have come men and women who have made history, made the world brighter, better, higher, holier for their existence in it, made of it a place good to live in and worthy to die in,—men and women who have hallowed it by their footsteps and sanctified it with their presence and in many cases consecrated it with their blood. Poverty is a blessing, not an evil, a benison from the Father's hand if accepted in the right spirit. Instead of retarding, it has elevated literature in all ages. Homer was a blind beggarman singing his snatches of song for the dole of charity; grand old Socrates, oracle of wisdom, many a day went without his dinner because he had not the wherewithal to get it, while teaching the youth of Athens. The divine Dante was nothing better than a beggar, houseless, homeless, friendless, wandering through Italy while he composed his immortal cantos. Milton, who in his blindness "looked where angels fear to tread," was steeped in poverty while writing his sublime conception, "Paradise Lost." Shakespeare was glad to hold and water the horses of patrons outside the White Horse Theatre for a few pennies in order to buy bread. Burns burst forth in never-dying song while guiding the ploughshare. Poor Heinrich Heine, neglected and in poverty, from his "mattress grave" of suffering in Paris added literary laurels to the wreath of his German Fatherland. In America Elihu Burritt, while attending the anvil, made himself a master of a score of languages and became the literary lion of his age and country.

In other fields of endeavor poverty has been the spur to action. Napoleon was born in obscurity, the son of a hand-to-mouth scrivener in the backward island of Corsica. Abraham Lincoln, the boast and pride of America, the man who made this land too hot for the feet of slaves, came from a log cabin in the Ohio backwoods. So did James A. Garfield. Ulysses Grant came from a tanyard to become the world's greatest general. Thomas A. Edison commenced as a newsboy on a railway train.

The examples of these men are incentives to action. Poverty thrust them forward instead of keeping them back. Therefore, if you are poor make your circumstances a means to an end. Have ambition, keep a goal in sight and bend every energy to reach that goal. A story is told of Thomas Carlyle the day he attained the highest honor the literary world could confer upon him when he was elected Lord Rector of Edinburgh University. After his installation speech, in going through the halls, he met a student seemingly deep in study. In his own peculiar, abrupt, crusty way the Sage of Chelsea interrogated the young man: "For what profession are you studying?" "I don't know," returned the youth. "You don't know," thundered Carlyle, "young man, you are a fool." Then he went on to qualify his vehement remark, "My boy when I was your age, I was stooped in grinding, gripping poverty in the little village of Ecclefechan, in the wilds of [Transcriber's note: First part of word illegible]-frieshire, where in all the place only the minister and myself could read the Bible, yet poor and obscure as I was, in my mind's eye I saw a chair awaiting for me in the Temple of Fame and day and night and night and day I studied until I sat in that chair to-day as Lord Rector of Edinburgh University."

Another Scotchman, Robert Buchanan, the famous novelist, set out for London from Glasgow with but half-a-crown in his pocket. "Here goes," said he, "for a grave in Westminster Abbey." He was not much of a scholar, but his ambition carried him on and he became one of the great literary lions of the world's metropolis.

Henry M. Stanley was a poorhouse waif whose real name was John Rowlands. He was brought up in a Welsh workhouse, but he had ambition, so he rose to be a great explorer, a great writer, became a member of Parliament and was knighted by the British Sovereign.

Have ambition to succeed and you will succeed. Cut the word "failure" out of your lexicon. Don't acknowledge it. Remember

```
"In life's earnest battle they only prevail
 Who daily march onward and never say fail."
```

Let every obstacle you encounter be but a stepping stone in the path of onward progress to the goal of success.

If untoward circumstances surround you, resolve to overcome them. Bunyan wrote the "Pilgrim's Progress" in Bedford jail on scraps of wrapping paper while he was half starved on a diet of bread and water. That unfortunate American genius, Edgar Allan Poe, wrote "The Raven," the most wonderful conception as well as the most highly artistic poem in all English literature, in a little cottage in the Fordham section of New York while he was in the direst straits of want. Throughout all his short and wonderfully brilliant career, poor Poe never had a dollar he could call his own. Such, however, was both his fault and his misfortune and he is a bad exemplar.

Don't think that the knowledge of a library of books is essential to success as a writer. Often a multiplicity of books is confusing. Master a few good books and master them well and you will have all that is necessary. A great authority has said: "Beware of the man of one book," which means that a man of one book is a master of the craft. It is claimed that a thorough knowledge of the Bible alone will make any person a master of literature. Certain it is that the Bible and Shakespeare constitute an epitome of the essentials of knowledge. Shakespeare gathered the fruitage of all who went before him, he has sown the seeds for all who shall ever come after him. He was the great intellectual ocean whose waves touch the continents of all thought.

Books are cheap now-a-days, the greatest works, thanks to the printing press, are within the reach of all, and the more you read, the better, provided they are worth reading. Sometimes a man takes poison into his system unconscious of the fact that it is poison, as in the case of certain foods, and it is very hard to throw off its effects. Therefore, be careful in your choice of reading matter. If you cannot afford a full library, and as has been said, such is not necessary, select a few of the great works of the master minds, assimilate and digest them, so that they will be of advantage to your literary system. Elsewhere in this volume is given a list of some of the world's masterpieces from which you can make a selection.

Your brain is a storehouse, don't put useless furniture into it to crowd it to the exclusion of what is useful. Lay up only the valuable and serviceable kind which you can call into requisition at any moment.

As it is necessary to study the best authors in order to be a writer, so it is necessary to study the best speakers in order to talk with correctness and in good style. To talk rightly you must imitate the masters of oral speech. Listen to the best conversationalists and how they express themselves. Go to hear the leading lectures, speeches and sermons. No need to imitate the gestures of elocution, it is nature, not art, that makes the elocutionist and the orator. It is not *how* a speaker expresses himself but the language which he uses and the manner of its use which should interest you. Have you heard the present day masters of speech? There have been past time masters but their tongues are stilled in the dust of the grave, and you can only read their eloquence now. You can, however, listen to the charm of the living. To many of us voices still speak from the grave, voices to which we have listened when fired with the divine essence of speech. Perhaps you have hung with rapture on the words of Beecher and Talmage. Both thrilled the souls of men and won countless thousands over to a living gospel. Both were masters of words, they scattered the flowers of rhetoric on the shrine of eloquence and hurled veritable bouquets at their audiences which were eagerly seized by the latter and treasured in the storehouse of memory. Both were scholars and philosophers, yet they were far surpassed by Spurgeon, a plain man of the people with little or no claim to education in the modern sense of the word. Spurgeon by his speech attracted thousands to his Tabernacle. The Protestant and Catholic, Turk, Jew and Mohammedan rushed to hear him and listened, entranced, to his language. Such another was Dwight L. Moody, the greatest Evangelist the world has ever known. Moody was not a man of learning; he commenced life as a shoe salesman in Chicago, yet no man ever lived who drew such audiences and so fascinated them with the spell of his speech. "Oh, that was personal magnetism," you will say, but it was nothing of the kind. It was the burning words that fell from the lips of these men, and the way, the manner, the force with which they used those words that counted and attracted the crowds to listen unto them. Personal magnetism or personal appearance entered not as factors into their success. Indeed as far as physique were concerned, some of them were handicapped. Spurgeon was a short, podgy, fat little man, Moody was like a country farmer, Talmage in his big cloak was one of the most slovenly of men and only Beecher was passable in the way of refinement and gentlemanly bearing. Physical appearance, as so many think, is not the sesame to the interest of an audience. Daniel O'Connell, the Irish tribune, was a homely, ugly, awkward, ungainly man, yet his words attracted millions to his side and gained for him the hostile ear of the British Parliament, he was a master of verbiage and knew just what to say to captivate his audiences.

It is words and their placing that count on almost all occasions. No matter how refined in other respects the person may be, if he use words wrongly and express himself in language not in accordance with a proper construction, he will repel you, whereas the man who places his words correctly and employs language in harmony with the laws of good speech, let him be ever so humble, will attract and have an influence over you.

The good speaker, the correct speaker, is always able to command attention and doors are thrown open to him which remain closed to others not equipped with a like facility of expression. The man who can talk well and to the point need never fear to go idle. He is required in nearly every walk of life and field of human endeavor, the world wants him at every turn. Employers are constantly on the lookout for good talkers, those who are able to attract the public and convince others by the force of their language. A man may be able, educated, refined, of unblemished character, nevertheless if he lack the power to express himself, put forth his views in good and appropriate speech he has to take a back seat, while some one with much less ability gets the opportunity to come to the front because he can clothe his ideas in ready words and talk effectively.

You may again say that nature, not art, makes a man a fluent speaker; to a great degree this is true, but it is *art* that makes him a *correct* speaker, and correctness leads to fluency. It is possible for everyone to become a correct speaker if he will but persevere and take a little pains and care.

At the risk of repetition good advice may be here emphasized: Listen to the best speakers and note carefully the words which impress you most. Keep a notebook and jot down words, phrases, sentences that are in any way striking or out of the ordinary run. If you do not understand the exact meaning of a word you have heard, look it up in the dictionary. There are many words, called synonyms, which have almost a like signification, nevertheless, when examined they express different shades of meaning and in some cases, instead of being close related, are widely divergent. Beware of such words, find their exact meaning and learn to use them in their right places.

Be open to criticism, don't resent it but rather invite it and look upon those as friends who point out your defects in order that you may remedy them.

CHAPTER XI

SLANG

Origin—American Slang—Foreign Slang

Slang is more or less common in nearly all ranks of society and in every walk of life at the present day. Slang words and expressions have crept into our everyday language, and so insiduously, that they have not been detected by the great majority of speakers, and so have become part and parcel of their vocabulary on an equal footing with the legitimate words of speech. They are called upon to do similar service as the ordinary words used in everyday conversation—to express thoughts and desires and convey meaning from one to another. In fact, in some cases, slang has become so useful that it has far outstripped classic speech and made for itself such a position in the vernacular that it would be very hard in some cases to get along without it. Slang words have usurped the place of regular words of language in very many instances and reign supreme in their own strength and influence.

Cant and slang are often confused in the popular mind, yet they are not synonymous, though very closely allied, and proceeding from a common Gypsy origin. Cant is the language of a certain class —the peculiar phraseology or dialect of a certain craft, trade or profession, and is not readily understood save by the initiated of such craft, trade or profession. It may be correct, according to the rules of grammar, but it is not universal; it is confined to certain parts and localities and is only intelligible to those for whom it is intended. In short, it is an esoteric language which only the initiated can understand. The jargon, or patter, of thieves is cant and it is only understood by thieves who have been let into its significance; the initiated language of professional gamblers is cant, and is only intelligible to gamblers.

On the other hand, slang, as it is nowadays, belongs to no particular class but is scattered all over and gets *entre* into every kind of society and is understood by all where it passes current in everyday expression. Of course, the nature of the slang, to a great extent, depends upon the locality, as it chiefly is concerned with colloquialisms or words and phrases common to a particular section. For instance, the slang of London is slightly different from that of New York, and some words in the one city may be unintelligible in the other, though well understood in that in which they are current. Nevertheless, slang may be said to be universally understood. "To kick the bucket," "to cross the Jordan," "to hop the twig" are just as expressive of the departing from life in the backwoods of America or the wilds of Australia as they are in London or Dublin.

Slang simply consists of words and phrases which pass current but are not refined, nor elegant enough, to be admitted into polite speech or literature whenever they are recognized as such. But, as has been said, a great many use slang without their knowing it as slang and incorporate it into their everyday speech and conversation.

Some authors purposely use slang to give emphasis and spice in familiar and humorous writing, but they should not be imitated by the tyro. A master, such as Dickens, is forgivable, but in the novice it is unpardonable.

There are several kinds of slang attached to different professions and classes of society. For instance, there is college slang, political slang, sporting slang, etc. It is the nature of slang to circulate freely among all classes, yet there are several kinds of this current form of language corresponding to the several classes of society. The two great divisions of slang are the vulgar of the uneducated and coarse-minded, and the high-toned slang of the so-called upper classes—the educated and the wealthy. The hoyden of the gutter does not use the same slang as my lady in her boudoir, but both use it, and so expressive is it that the one might readily understand the other if brought in contact. Therefore, there are what may be styled an ignorant slang and an educated slang —the one common to the purlieus and the alleys, the other to the parlor and the drawing-room.

In all cases the object of slang is to express an idea in a more vigorous, piquant and terse manner than standard usage ordinarily admits. A school girl, when she wants to praise a baby, exclaims: "Oh, isn't he awfully cute!" To say that he is very nice would be too weak a way to express her admiration. When a handsome girl appears on the street an enthusiastic masculine admirer, to express his appreciation of her beauty, tells you: "She is a peach, a bird, a cuckoo," any of which accentuates his estimation of the young lady and is much more emphatic than saying: "She is a beautiful girl," "a handsome maiden," or "lovely young woman."

When a politician defeats his rival he will tell you "it was a cinch," he had a "walk-over," to impress you how easy it was to gain the victory.

Some slang expressions are of the nature of metaphors and are highly figurative. Such are "to pass in your checks," "to hold up," "to pull the wool over your eyes," "to talk through your hat," "to fire out," "to go back on," "to make yourself solid with," "to have a jag on," "to be loaded," "to freeze on to," "to bark up the wrong tree," "don't monkey with the buzz-saw," and "in the soup." Most slang had a bad origin. The greater part originated in the cant of thieves' Latin, but it broke away from this cant of malefactors in time and gradually evolved itself from its unsavory past until it developed into a current form of expressive speech. Some slang, however, can trace its origin back to very respectable sources.

"Stolen fruits are sweet" may be traced to the Bible in sentiment. Proverbs, ix:17 has it: "Stolen waters are sweet." "What are you giving me," supposed to be a thorough Americanism, is based upon Genesis, xxxviii:16. The common slang, "a bad man," in referring to Western desperadoes, in almost the identical sense now used, is found in Spenser's *Faerie Queen,* Massinger's play *"A New Way to Pay Old Debts,"* and in Shakespeare's *"King Henry VIII."* The expression "to blow on," meaning to inform, is in Shakespeare's *"As You Like it."* "It's all Greek to me" is traceable to the play of *"Julius Caesar."* "All cry and no wool" is in Butler's *"Hudibras."* "Pious frauds," meaning hypocrites, is from the same source. "Too thin," referring to an excuse, is from Smollett's *"Peregrine Pickle."* Shakespeare also used it.

America has had a large share in contributing to modern slang. "The heathen Chinee," and "Ways that are dark, and tricks that are vain," are from Bret Harte's *Truthful James.* "Not for Joe," arose during the Civil War when one soldier refused to give a drink to another. "Not if I know myself" had its origin in Chicago. "What's the matter with——? He's all right," had its beginning in Chicago also and first was "What's the matter with Hannah." referring to a lazy domestic servant. "There's millions in it," and "By a large majority" come from Mark Twain's *Gilded Age*. "Pull down your vest," "jim-jams," "got 'em bad," "that's what's the matter," "go hire a hall," "take in your sign," "dry up," "hump yourself," "it's the man around the corner," "putting up a job," "put a head on him," "no back talk," "bottom dollar," "went off on his ear," "chalk it down," "staving him off," "making it warm," "dropping him gently," "dead gone," "busted," "counter jumper," "put up or shut up," "bang up," "smart Aleck," "too much jaw," "chin-music," "top heavy," "barefooted on the top of the head," "a little too fresh," "champion liar," "chief cook and bottle washer," "bag and baggage," "as fine as silk," "name your poison," "died with his boots on," "old hoss," "hunkey dorey," "hold your horses," "galoot" and many others in use at present are all Americanisms in slang.

California especially has been most fecund in this class of figurative language. To this State we owe "go off and die," "don't you forget it," "rough deal," "square deal," "flush times," "pool your issues," "go bury yourself," "go drown yourself," "give your tongue a vacation," "a bad egg," "go climb a tree," "plug hats," "Dolly Vardens," "well fixed," "down to bed rock," "hard pan," "pay dirt," "petered out," "it won't wash," "slug of whiskey," "it pans out well," and "I should smile." "Small potatoes, and few in the hill," "soft snap," "all fired," "gol durn it," "an up-hill job," "slick," "short cut," "guess not," "correct thing" are Bostonisms. The terms "innocent," "acknowledge the corn," "bark up the wrong tree," "great snakes," "I reckon," "playing 'possum," "dead shot," had their origin in the Southern States. "Doggone it," "that beats the Dutch," "you bet," "you bet your boots," sprang from New York. "Step down and out" originated in the Beecher trial, just as "brain-storm" originated in the Thaw trial.

Among the slang phrases that have come directly to us from England may be mentioned "throw up the sponge," "draw it mild," "give us a rest," "dead beat," "on the shelf," "up the spout," "stunning," "gift of the gab," etc.

The newspapers are responsible for a large part of the slang. Reporters, staff writers, and even editors, put words and phrases into the mouths of individuals which they never utter. New York is supposed to be the headquarters of slang, particularly that portion of it known as the Bowery. All transgressions and corruptions of language are supposed to originate in that unclassic section, while the truth is that the laws of polite English are as much violated on Fifth Avenue. Of course, the foreign element mincing their "pidgin" English have given the Bowery an unenviable reputation, but there are just as good speakers of the vernacular on the Bowery as elsewhere in the greater city. Yet every inexperienced newspaper reporter thinks that it is incumbent on him to hold the Bowery up to ridicule and laughter, so he sits down, and out of his circumscribed brain, mutilates the English tongue (he can rarely coin a word), and blames the mutilation on the Bowery.

'Tis the same with newspapers and authors, too, detracting the Irish race. Men and women who have never seen the green hills of Ireland, paint Irish characters as boors and blunderers and make them say ludicrous things and use such language as is never heard within the four walls of Ireland. 'Tis very well known that Ireland is the most learned country on the face of the earth—is, and has been. The schoolmaster has been abroad there for hundreds, almost thousands, of years, and nowhere else in the world to-day is the king's English spoken so purely as in the cities and towns of the little Western Isle.

Current events, happenings of everyday life, often give rise to slang words, and these, after a time, come into such general use that they take their places in everyday speech like ordinary words and, as has been said, their users forget that they once were slang. For instance, the days of the Land League in Ireland originated the word *boycott*, which was the name of a very unpopular landlord, Captain Boycott. The people refused to work for him, and his crops rotted on the ground. From this time any one who came into disfavor and whom his neighbors refused to assist in any way was said to be boycotted. Therefore to boycott means to punish by abandoning or depriving a person of the assistance of others. At first it was a notoriously slang word, but now it is standard in the English dictionaries.

Politics add to our slang words and phrases. From this source we get "dark horse," "the gray mare is the better horse," "barrel of money," "buncombe," "gerrymander," "scalawag," "henchman," "logrolling," "pulling the wires," "taking the stump," "machine," "slate," etc.

The money market furnishes us with "corner," "bull," "bear," "lamb," "slump," and several others.

The custom of the times and the requirements of current expression require the best of us to use slang words and phrases on occasions. Often we do not know they are slang, just as a child often uses profane words without consciousness of their being so. We should avoid the use of slang as much as possible, even when it serves to convey our ideas in a forceful manner. And when it has not gained a firm foothold in current speech it should be used not at all. Remember that most all slang is of vulgar origin and bears upon its face the bend sinister of vulgarity. Of the slang that is of good birth, pass it by if you can, for it is like a broken-down gentleman, of little good to any one. Imitate the great masters as much as you will in classical literature, but when it comes to their slang, draw the line. Dean Swift, the great Irish satirist, coined the word "phiz" for face. Don't imitate him. If you are speaking or writing of the beauty of a lady's face don't call it her "phiz." The Dean, as an intellectual giant, had a license to do so—you haven't. Shakespeare used the word "flush" to indicate plenty of money. Well, just remember there was only one Shakespeare, and he was the only one that had a right to use that word in that sense. You'll never be a Shakespeare, there will never be such another—Nature exhausted herself in producing him. Bulwer used the word "stretch" for hang, as to stretch his neck. Don't follow his example in such use of the word. Above all, avoid the low, coarse, vulgar slang, which is made to pass for wit among the riff-raff of the street. If you are speaking or writing of a person having died last night don't say or write: "He hopped the twig," or "he kicked the bucket." If you are compelled to listen to a person discoursing on a subject of which he knows little or nothing, don't say "He is talking through his hat." If you are telling of having shaken hands with Mr. Roosevelt don't say "He tipped me his flipper." If you are speaking of a wealthy man don't say "He has plenty of spondulix," or "the long green." All such slang is low, coarse and vulgar and is to be frowned upon on any and every occasion.

If you use slang use the refined kind and use it like a gentleman, that it will not hurt or give offense to any one. Cardinal Newman defined a gentleman as he who never inflicts pain. Be a gentleman in your slang—never inflict pain.

CHAPTER XII

WRITING FOR NEWSPAPERS

Qualification—Appropriate Subjects—Directions

The newspaper nowadays goes into every home in the land; what was formerly regarded as a luxury is now looked upon as a necessity. No matter how poor the individual, he is not too poor to afford a penny to learn, not alone what is taking place around him in his own immediate vicinity, but also what is happening in every quarter of the globe. The laborer on the street can be as well posted on the news of the day as the banker in his office. Through the newspaper he can feel the pulse of the country and find whether its vitality is increasing or diminishing; he can read the signs of the times and scan the political horizon for what concerns his own interests. The doings of foreign countries are spread before him and he can see at a glance the occurrences in the remotest corners of earth. If a fire occurred in London last night he can read about it at his breakfast table in New York this morning, and probably get a better account than the Londoners themselves. If a duel takes place in Paris he can read all about it even before the contestants have left the field.

There are upwards of 3,000 daily newspapers in the United States, more than 2,000 of which are published in towns containing less than 100,000 inhabitants. In fact, many places of less than 10,000 population can boast the publishing of a daily newspaper. There are more than 15,000 weeklies published. Some of the so-called country papers wield quite an influence in their localities, and even outside, and are money-making agencies for their owners and those connected with them, both by way of circulation and advertisements.

It is surprising the number of people in this country who make a living in the newspaper field. Apart from the regular toilers there are thousands of men and women who make newspaper work a side issue, who add tidy sums of "pin money" to their incomes by occasional contributions to the daily, weekly and monthly press. Most of these people are only persons of ordinary, everyday ability, having just enough education to express themselves intelligently in writing.

It is a mistake to imagine, as so many do, that an extended education is necessary for newspaper work. Not at all! On the contrary, in some cases, a high-class education is a hindrance, not a help in this direction. The general newspaper does not want learned disquisitions nor philosophical theses; as its name implies, it wants news, current news, interesting news, something to appeal to its readers, to arouse them and rivet their attention. In this respect very often a boy can write a better article than a college professor. The professor would be apt to use words beyond the capacity of most of the readers, while the boy, not knowing such words, would probably simply tell what he saw, how great the damage was, who were killed or injured, etc., and use language which all would understand.

Of course, there are some brilliant scholars, deeply-read men and women in the newspaper realm, but, on the whole, those who have made the greatest names commenced ignorant enough and most of them graduated by way of the country paper. Some of the leading writers of England and America at the present time started their literary careers by contributing to the rural press. They perfected and polished themselves as they went along until they were able to make names for themselves in universal literature.

If you want to contribute to newspapers or enter the newspaper field as a means of livelihood, don't let lack of a college or university education stand in your way. As has been said elsewhere in this book, some of the greatest masters of English literature were men who had but little advantage in the way of book learning. Shakespeare, Bunyan, Burns, and scores of others, who have left their names indelibly inscribed on the tablets of fame, had little to boast of in the way of book education, but they had what is popularly known as "horse" sense and a good working knowledge of the world; in other words, they understood human nature, and were natural themselves. Shakespeare understood mankind because he was himself a man; hence he has portrayed the feelings, the emotions, the passions with a master's touch, delineating the king in his palace as true to nature as he has done the peasant in his hut. The monitor within his own breast gave him warning as to what was right and what was wrong, just as the daemon ever by the side of old Socrates whispered in his ear the course to pursue under any and all circumstances. Burns guiding the plough conceived thoughts and clothed them in a language which has never, nor probably never will be, surpassed by all the learning which art can confer. These men were natural, and it was the perfection of this naturality that wreathed their brows with the never-fading laurels of undying fame.

If you would essay to write for the newspaper you must be natural and express yourself in your accustomed way without putting on airs or frills; you must not ape ornaments and indulge in bombast or rhodomontade which stamp a writer as not only superficial but silly. There is no room for such in the everyday newspaper. It wants facts stated in plain, unvarnished, unadorned language. True, you should read the best authors and, as far as possible, imitate their style, but don't try to literally copy them. Be yourself on every occasion—no one else.

```
Not like Homer would I write,
Not like Dante if I might,
Not like Shakespeare at his best,
Not like Goethe or the rest,
Like myself, however small,
Like myself, or not at all.
```

Put yourself in place of the reader and write what will interest yourself and in such a way that your language will appeal to your own ideas of the fitness of things. You belong to the *great* commonplace majority, therefore don't forget that in writing for the newspapers you are writing for that majority and not for the learned and aesthetic minority.

Remember you are writing for the man on the street and in the street car, you want to interest him, to compel him to read what you have to say. He does not want a display of learning; he wants news about something which concerns himself, and you must tell it to him in a plain, simple manner just as you would do if you were face to face with him.

What can you write about? Why about anything that will constitute current news, some leading event of the day, anything that will appeal to the readers of the paper to which you wish to submit it. No matter in what locality you may live, however backward it may be, you can always find something of genuine human interest to others. If there is no news happening, write of something that appeals to yourself. We are all constituted alike, and the chances are that what will interest you will interest others. Descriptions of adventure are generally acceptable. Tell of a fox hunt, or a badger hunt, or a bear chase.

If there is any important manufacturing plant in your neighborhood describe it and, if possible, get photographs, for photography plays a very important part in the news items of to-day. If a "great" man lives near you, one whose name is on the tip of every tongue, go and get an interview with him, obtain his views on the public questions of the day, describe his home life and his surroundings and how he spends his time.

Try and strike something germane to the moment, something that stands out prominently in the limelight of the passing show. If a noted personage, some famous man or woman, is visiting the country, it is a good time to write up the place from which he or she comes and the record he or she has made there. For instance, it was opportune to write of Sulu and the little Pacific archipelago during the Sultan's trip through the country. If an attempt is made to blow up an American battleship, say, in the harbor of Appia, in Samoa, it affords a chance to write about Samoa and Robert Louis Stephenson. When Manuel was hurled from the throne of Portugal it was a ripe time to write of Portugal and Portuguese affairs. If any great occurrence is taking place in a foreign country such as the crowning of a king or the dethronement of a monarch, it is a good time to write up the history of the country and describe the events leading up to the main issue. When a particularly savage outbreak occurs amongst wild tribes in the dependencies, such as a rising of the Manobos in the Philippines, it is opportune to write of such tribes and their surroundings, and the causes leading up to the revolt.

Be constantly on the lookout for something that will suit the passing hour, read the daily papers and probably in some obscure corner you may find something that will serve you as a foundation for a good article—something, at least, that will give you a clue.

Be circumspect in your selection of a paper to which to submit your copy. Know the tone and general import of the paper, its social leanings and political affiliations, also its religious sentiments, and, in fact, all the particulars you can regarding it. It would be injudicious for you to send an article on a prize fight to a religious paper or, *vice versa.*

If you get your copy back don't be disappointed nor yet disheartened. Perseverance counts more in the newspaper field than anywhere else, and only perseverance wins in the long run. You must become resilient; if you are pressed down, spring up again. No matter how many rebuffs you may receive, be not discouraged but call fresh energy to your assistance and make another stand. If the right stuff is in you it is sure to be discovered; your light will not remain long hidden under a bushel in the newspaper domain. If you can deliver the goods editors will soon be begging you instead of your begging them. Those men are constantly on the lookout for persons who can make good.

Once you get into print the battle is won, for it will be an incentive to you to persevere and improve yourself at every turn. Go over everything you write, cut and slash and prune until you get it into as perfect form as possible. Eliminate every superfluous word and be careful to strike out all ambiguous expressions and references.

If you are writing for a weekly paper remember it differs from a daily one. Weeklies want what will not alone interest the man on the street, but the woman at the fireside; they want out-of-the-way facts, curious scraps of lore, personal notes of famous or eccentric people, reminiscences of exciting experiences, interesting gleanings in life's numberless by-ways, in short, anything that will entertain, amuse, instruct the home circle. There is always something occurring in your immediate surroundings, some curious event or thrilling episode that will furnish you with data for an article. You must know the nature of the weekly to which you submit your copy the same as you must know the daily.

The monthlies offer another attractive field for the literary aspirant. Here, again, don't think you must be an university professor to write for a monthly magazine. Many, indeed most, of the foremost magazine contributors are men and women who have never passed through a college except by going in at the front door and emerging from the back one. However, for the most part, they are individuals of wide experience who know the practical side of life as distinguished from the theoretical.

The ordinary monthly magazine treats of the leading questions and issues which are engaging the attention of the world for the moment, great inventions, great discoveries, whatever is engrossing the popular mind for the time being, such as flying machines, battleships, sky-scrapers, the opening of mines, the development of new lands, the political issues, views of party leaders, character sketches of distinguished personages, etc. However, before trying your skill for a monthly magazine it would be well for you to have a good apprenticeship in writing for the daily press.

Above all things, remember that perseverance is the key that opens the door of success. Persevere! If you are turned down don't get disheartened; on the contrary, let the rebuff act as a stimulant to further effort. Many of the most successful writers of our time have been turned down again and again. For days and months, and even years, some of them have hawked their wares from one literary door to another until they found a purchaser. You may be a great writer in embryo, but you will never develop into a fetus, not to speak of full maturity, unless you bring out what is in you. Give yourself a chance to grow and seize upon everything that will enlarge the scope of your horizon. Keep your eyes wide open and there is not a moment of the day in which you will not see something to interest you and in which you may be able to interest others. Learn, too, how to read Nature's book. There's a lesson in everything—in the stones, the grass, the trees, the babbling brooks and the singing birds. Interpret the lesson for yourself, then teach it to others. Always be in earnest in your writing; go about it in a determined kind of way, don't be faint-hearted or backward, be brave, be brave, and evermore be brave.

```
On the wide, tented field in the battle of life,
   With an army of millions before you;
Like a hero of old gird your soul for the strife
   And let not the foeman tramp o'er you;
Act, act like a soldier and proudly rush on
   The most valiant in Bravery's van,
With keen, flashing sword cut your way to the front
   And show to the world you're a Man.
```

If you are of the masculine gender be a man in all things in the highest and best acceptation of the word. That is the noblest title you can boast, higher far than that of earl or duke, emperor or king. In the same way womanhood is the grandest crown the feminine head can wear. When the world frowns on you and everything seems to go wrong, possess your soul in patience and hope for the dawn of a brighter day. It will come. The sun is always shining behind the darkest clouds. When you get your manuscripts back again and again, don't despair, nor think the editor cruel and unkind. He, too, has troubles of his own. Keep up your spirits until you have made the final test and put your talents to a last analysis, then if you find you cannot get into print be sure that newspaper writing or literary work is not your *forte*, and turn to something else. If nothing better presents itself, try shoemaking or digging ditches. Remember honest labor, no matter how humble, is ever dignified. If you are a woman throw aside the pen, sit down and darn your brother's, your father's, or your husband's socks, or put on a calico apron, take soap and water and scrub the floor. No matter who you are do something useful. That old sophistry about the world owing you a living has been exploded long ago. The world does not owe you a living, but you owe it servitude, and if you do not pay the debt you are not serving the purpose of an all-wise Providence and filling the place for which you were created. It is for you to serve the world, to make it better, brighter, higher, holier, grander, nobler, richer, for your having lived in it. This you can do in no matter what position fortune has cast you, whether it be that of street laborer or president. Fight the good fight and gain the victory.

```
"Above all, to thine own self be true,
 And 'twill follow as the night the
 day, Thou canst not then be false to any man."
```

CHAPTER XIII

CHOICE OF WORDS

Small Words—Their Importance—The Anglo-Saxon Element

In another place in this book advice has been given to never use a long word when a short one will serve the same purpose. This advice is to be emphasized. Words of "learned length and thundering sound" should be avoided on all possible occasions. They proclaim shallowness of intellect and vanity of mind. The great purists, the masters of diction, the exemplars of style, used short, simple words that all could understand; words about which there could be no ambiguity as to meaning. It must be remembered that by our words we teach others; therefore, a very great responsibility rests upon us in regard to the use of a right language. We must take care that we think and speak in a way so clear that there may be no misapprehension or danger of conveying wrong impressions by vague and misty ideas enunciated in terms which are liable to be misunderstood by those whom we address. Words give a body or form to our ideas, without which they are apt to be so foggy that we do not see where they are weak or false. We must make the endeavor to employ such words as will put the idea we have in our own mind into the mind of another. This is the greatest art in the world —to clothe our ideas in words clear and comprehensive to the intelligence of others. It is the art which the teacher, the minister, the lawyer, the orator, the business man, must master if they would command success in their various fields of endeavor. It is very hard to convey an idea to, and impress it on, another when he has but a faint conception of the language in which the idea is expressed; but it is impossible to convey it at all when the words in which it is clothed are unintelligible to the listener.

If we address an audience of ordinary men and women in the English language, but use such words as they cannot comprehend, we might as well speak to them in Coptic or Chinese, for they will derive no benefit from our address, inasmuch as the ideas we wish to convey are expressed in words which communicate no intelligent meaning to their minds.

Long words, learned words, words directly derived from other languages are only understood by those who have had the advantages of an extended education. All have not had such advantages. The great majority in this grand and glorious country of ours have to hustle for a living from an early age. Though education is free, and compulsory also, very many never get further than the "Three R's." These are the men with whom we have to deal most in the arena of life, the men with the horny palms and the iron muscles, the men who build our houses, construct our railroads, drive our street cars and trains, till our fields, harvest our crops—in a word, the men who form the foundation of all society, the men on whom the world depends to make its wheels go round. The language of the colleges and universities is not for them and they can get along very well without it; they have no need for it at all in their respective callings. The plain, simple words of everyday life, to which the common people have been used around their own firesides from childhood, are the words we must use in our dealings with them.

Such words are understood by them and understood by the learned as well; why then not use them universally and all the time? Why make a one-sided affair of language by using words which only one class of the people, the so-called learned class, can understand? Would it not be better to use, on all occasions, language which the both classes can understand? If we take the trouble to investigate we shall find that the men who exerted the greatest sway over the masses and the multitude as orators, lawyers, preachers and in other public capacities, were men who used very simple language. Daniel Webster was among the greatest orators this country has produced. He touched the hearts of senates and assemblages, of men and women with the burning eloquence of his words. He never used a long word when he could convey the same, or nearly the same, meaning with a short one. When he made a speech he always told those who put it in form for the press to strike out every long word. Study his speeches, go over all he ever said or wrote, and you will find that his language was always made up of short, clear, strong terms, although at times, for the sake of sound and oratorical effect, he was compelled to use a rather long word, but it was always against his inclination to do so, and where was the man who could paint, with words, as Webster painted! He could picture things in a way so clear that those who heard him felt that they had seen that of which he spoke.

Abraham Lincoln was another who stirred the souls of men, yet he was not an orator, not a scholar; he did not write M.A. or Ph.D. after his name, or any other college degree, for he had none. He graduated from the University of Hard Knocks, and he never forgot this severe *Alma Mater* when he became President of the United States. He was just as plain, I just as humble, as in the days when he split rails or plied a boat on the Sangamon. He did not use big words, but he used the words of the people, and in such a way as to make them beautiful. His Gettysburg address is an English classic, one of the great masterpieces of the language.

From the mere fact that a word is short it does not follow that it is always clear, but it is true that nearly all clear words are short, and that most of the long words, especially those which we get from other languages, are misunderstood to a great extent by the ordinary rank and file of the people. Indeed, it is to be doubted if some of the "scholars" using them, fully understand their import on occasions. A great many such words admit of several interpretations. A word has to be in use a great deal before people get thoroughly familiar with its meaning. Long words, not alone obscure thought and make the ideas hazy, but at times they tend to mix up things in such a way that positively harmful results follow from their use.

For instance, crime can be so covered with the folds of long words as to give it a different appearance. Even the hideousness of sin can be cloaked with such words until its outlines look like a thing of beauty. When a bank cashier makes off with a hundred thousand dollars we politely term his crime *defalcation* instead of plain *theft*, and instead of calling himself a *thief* we grandiosely allude to him as a *defaulter*. When we see a wealthy man staggering along a fashionable thoroughfare under the influence of alcohol, waving his arms in the air and shouting boisterously, we smile and say, poor gentleman, he is somewhat *exhilarated;* or at worst we say, he is slightly *inebriated;* but when we see a poor man who has fallen from grace by putting an "enemy into his mouth to steal away his brain" we express our indignation in the simple language of the words: "Look at the wretch; he is dead drunk."

When we find a person in downright lying we cover the falsehood with the finely-spun cloak of the word *prevarication*. Shakespeare says, "a rose by any other name would smell as sweet," and by a similar sequence, a lie, no matter by what name you may call it, is always a lie and should be condemned; then why not simply call it a lie? Mean what you say and say what you mean; call a spade a spade, it is the best term you can apply to the implement.

When you try to use short words and shun long ones in a little while you will find that you can do so with ease. A farmer was showing a horse to a city-bred gentleman. The animal was led into a paddock in which an old sow-pig was rooting. "What a fine quadruped!" exclaimed the city man.

"Which of the two do you mean, the pig or the horse?" queried the farmer, "for, in my opinion, both of them are fine quadrupeds."

Of course the visitor meant the horse, so it would have been much better had he called the animal by its simple; ordinary name—, there would have been no room for ambiguity in his remark. He profited, however, by the incident, and never called a horse a quadruped again.

Most of the small words, the simple words, the beautiful words which express so much within small bounds belong to the pure Anglo-Saxon element of our language. This element has given names to the heavenly bodies, the sun, moon and stars; to three out of the four elements, earth, fire and water; three out of the four seasons, spring, summer and winter. Its simple words are applied to all the natural divisions of time, except one, as day, night, morning, evening, twilight, noon, mid-day, midnight, sunrise and sunset. The names of light, heat, cold, frost, rain, snow, hail, sleet, thunder, lightning, as well as almost all those objects which form the component parts of the beautiful, as expressed in external scenery, such as sea and land, hill and dale, wood and stream, etc., are Anglo-Saxon. To this same language we are indebted for those words which express the earliest and dearest connections, and the strongest and most powerful feelings of Nature, and which, as a consequence, are interwoven with the fondest and most hallowed associations. Of such words are father, mother, husband, wife, brother, sister, son, daughter, child, home, kindred, friend, hearth, roof and fireside.

The chief emotions of which we are susceptible are expressed in the same language—love, hope, fear, sorrow, shame, and also the outward signs by which these emotions are indicated, as tear, smile, laugh, blush, weep, sigh, groan. Nearly all our national proverbs are Anglo-Saxon. Almost all the terms and phrases by which we most energetically express anger, contempt and indignation are of the same origin.

What are known as the Smart Set and so-called polite society, are relegating a great many of our old Anglo-Saxon words into the shade, faithful friends who served their ancestors well. These self-appointed arbiters of diction regard some of the Anglo-Saxon words as too coarse, too plebeian for their aesthetic tastes and refined ears, so they are eliminating them from their vocabulary and replacing them with mongrels of foreign birth and hybrids of unknown origin. For the ordinary people, however, the man in the street or in the field, the woman in the kitchen or in the factory, they are still tried and true and, like old friends, should be cherished and preferred to all strangers, no matter from what source the latter may spring.

CHAPTER XIV

ENGLISH LANGUAGE

Beginning—Different Sources—The Present

The English language is the tongue now current in England and her colonies throughout the world and also throughout the greater part of the United States of America. It sprang from the German tongue spoken by the Teutons, who came over to Britain after the conquest of that country by the Romans. These Teutons comprised Angles, Saxons, Jutes and several other tribes from the northern part of Germany. They spoke different dialects, but these became blended in the new country, and the composite tongue came to be known as the Anglo-Saxon which has been the main basis for the language as at present constituted and is still the prevailing element. Therefore those who are trying to do away with some of the purely Anglo-Saxon words, on the ground that they are not refined enough to express their aesthetic ideas, are undermining main props which are necessary for the support of some important parts in the edifice of the language.

The Anglo-Saxon element supplies the essential parts of speech, the article, pronoun of all kinds, the preposition, the auxiliary verbs, the conjunctions, and the little particles which bind words into sentences and form the joints, sinews and ligaments of the language. It furnishes the most indispensable words of the vocabulary. (See Chap. XIII.) Nowhere is the beauty of Anglo-Saxon better illustrated than in the Lord's Prayer. Fifty-four words are pure Saxon and the remaining ones could easily be replaced by Saxon words. The gospel of St. John is another illustration of the almost exclusive use of Anglo-Saxon words. Shakespeare, at his best, is Anglo-Saxon. Here is a quotation from the *Merchant of Venice*, and of the fifty-five words fifty-two are Anglo-Saxon, the remaining three French:

```
All that glitters is not gold—
Often have you heard that told;
  Many a man his life hath sold,
  But my outside to behold.
Guilded tombs do worms infold.
  Had you been as wise as bold,
  Young in limbs, in judgment old,
  Your answer had not been inscrolled—
Fare you well, your suit is cold.
```

The lines put into the mouth of Hamlet's father in fierce intenseness, second only to Dante's inscription on the gate of hell, have one hundred and eight Anglo-Saxon and but fifteen Latin words.

The second constituent element of present English is Latin which comprises those words derived directly from the old Roman and those which came indirectly through the French.

The largest class of Latin words are those which came through the Norman-French, or Romance. The French Latinisms can be distinguished by the spelling. Thus Saviour comes from the Latin *Salvator* through the French *Sauveur*; judgment from the Latin *judiclum* through the French *jugement*; people, from the Latin *populus*, through the French *peuple*, etc.

For a long time the Saxon and Norman tongues refused to coalesce and were like two distinct currents flowing in different directions. Norman was spoken by the lords and barons in their feudal castles, in parliament and in the courts of justice. Saxon by the people in their rural homes, fields and workshops. For more than three hundred years the streams flowed apart, but finally they blended, taking in the Celtic and Danish elements, and as a result came the present English language with its simple system of grammatical inflection and its rich vocabulary.

The father of English prose is generally regarded as Wycliffe, who translated the Bible in 1380, while the paternal laurels in the secular poetical field are twined around the brows of Chaucer.

Besides the Germanic and Romanic, which constitute the greater part of the English language, many other tongues have furnished their quota. Of these the Celtic is perhaps the oldest. The Britons at Caesar's invasion, were a part of the Celtic family. The Celtic idiom is still spoken in two dialects, the Welsh in Wales, and the Gaelic in Ireland and the Highlands of Scotland. The Celtic words in English, are comparatively few; cart, dock, wire, rail, rug, cradle, babe, grown, griddle, lad, lass, are some in most common use.

The Danish element dates from the piratical invasions of the ninth and tenth centuries. It includes anger, awe, baffle, bang, bark, bawl, blunder, boulder, box, club, crash, dairy, dazzle, fellow, gable, gain, ill, jam, kidnap, kill, kidney, kneel, limber, litter, log, lull, lump, mast, mistake, nag, nasty, niggard, horse, plough, rug, rump, sale, scald, shriek, skin, skull, sledge, sleigh, tackle, tangle, tipple, trust, viking, window, wing, etc.

From the Hebrew we have a large number of proper names from Adam and Eve down to John and Mary and such words as Messiah, rabbi, hallelujah, cherub, seraph, hosanna, manna, satan, Sabbath, etc.

Many technical terms and names of branches of learning come from the Greek. In fact, nearly all the terms of learning and art, from the alphabet to the highest peaks of metaphysics and theology, come directly from the Greek—philosophy, logic, anthropology, psychology, aesthetics, grammar, rhetoric, history, philology, mathematics, arithmetic, astronomy, anatomy, geography, stenography, physiology, architecture, and hundreds more in similar domains; the subdivisions and ramifications of theology as exegesis, hermeneutics, apologetics, polemics, dogmatics, ethics, homiletics, etc., are all Greek.

The Dutch have given us some modern sea terms, as sloop, schooner, yacht and also a number of others as boom, bush, boor, brandy, duck, reef, skate, wagon. The Dutch of Manhattan island gave us boss, the name for employer or overseer, also cold slaa (cut cabbage and vinegar), and a number of geographical terms.

Many of our most pleasing euphonic words, especially in the realm of music, have been given to us directly from the Italian. Of these are piano, violin, orchestra, canto, allegro, piazza, gazette, umbrella, gondola, bandit, etc.

Spanish has furnished us with alligator, alpaca, bigot, cannibal, cargo, filibuster, freebooter, guano, hurricane, mosquito, negro, stampede, potato, tobacco, tomato, tariff, etc.

From Arabic we have several mathematical, astronomical, medical and chemical terms as alcohol, alcove, alembic, algebra, alkali, almanac, assassin, azure, cipher, elixir, harem, hegira, sofa, talisman, zenith and zero.

Bazaar, dervish, lilac, pagoda, caravan, scarlet, shawl, tartar, tiara and peach have come to us from the Persian.

Turban, tulip, divan and firman are Turkish.

Drosky, knout, rouble, steppe, ukase are Russian.

The Indians have helped us considerably and the words they have given us are extremely euphonic as exemplified in the names of many of our rivers and States, as Mississippi, Missouri, Minnehaha, Susquehanna, Monongahela, Niagara, Ohio, Massachusetts, Connecticut, Iowa, Nebraska, Dakota, etc. In addition to these proper names we have from the Indians wigwam, squaw, hammock, tomahawk, canoe, mocassin, hominy, etc.

There are many hybrid words in English, that is, words, springing from two or more different languages. In fact, English has drawn from all sources, and it is daily adding to its already large family, and not alone is it adding to itself, but it is spreading all over the world and promises to take in the entire human family beneath its folds ere long. It is the opinion of many that English, in a short time, will become the universal language. It is now being taught as a branch of the higher education in the best colleges and universities of Europe and in all commercial cities in every land throughout the world. In Asia it follows the British sway and the highways of commerce through the vast empire of East India with its two hundred and fifty millions of heathen and Mohammedan inhabitants. It is largely used in the seaports of Japan and China, and the number of natives of these countries who are learning it is increasing every day.

CHAPTER XV

MASTERS AND MASTERPIECES OF LITERATURE

Great Authors—Classification—The World's Best Books.

The Bible is the world's greatest book. Apart from its character as a work of divine revelation, it is the most perfect literature extant.

Leaving out the Bible the three greatest works are those of Homer, Dante and Shakespeare. These are closely followed by the works of Virgil and Milton.

INDISPENSABLE BOOKS

Homer, Dante, Cervantes, Shakespeare and Goethe.

(The best translation of *Homer* for the ordinary reader is by Chapman. Norton's translation of *Dante* and Taylor's translation of Goethe's *Faust* are recommended.)

A GOOD LIBRARY

Besides the works mentioned everyone should endeavor to have the following:

Plutarch's Lives, Meditations of Marcus Aurelius, Chaucer, Holy Living and Holy Dying (Jeremy Taylor), *Pilgrim's Progress, Macaulay's Essays, Bacon's Essays, Addison's Essays, Essays of Elia* (Charles Lamb), *Les Miserables* (Hugo), *Heroes and Hero Worship* (Carlyle), *Palgrave's Golden Treasury, Wordsworth, Vicar of Wakefield, Adam Bede* (George Eliot), *Vanity Fair* (Thackeray), *Ivanhoe* (Scott), *On the Heights* (Auerbach), *Eugenie Grandet* (Balzac), *Scarlet Letter* (Hawthorne), *Emerson's Essays, Boswell's Life of Johnson, History of the English People* (Green), *Outlines of Universal History, Origin of Species, Montaigne's Essays, Longfellow, Tennyson, Browning, Whittier, Ruskin, Herbert Spencer.*

A good encyclopoedia is very desirable and a reliable dictionary indispensable.

MASTERPIECES OF AMERICAN LITERATURE

Scarlet Letter, Parkman's Histories, Motley's Dutch Republic, Grant's Memoirs, Franklin's Autobiography, Webster's Speeches, Lowell's Bigelow Papers, also his *Critical Essays, Thoreau's Walden, Leaves of Grass* (Whitman), *Leather-stocking Tales* (Cooper), *Autocrat of the Breakfast Table, Ben Hur* and *Uncle Tom's Cabin.*

TEN GREATEST AMERICAN POETS

Bryant, Poe, Whittier, Longfellow, Lowell, Emerson, Whitman, Lanier, Aldrich and Stoddard.

TEN GREATEST ENGLISH POETS

Chaucer, Spenser, Shakespeare, Milton, Burns, Wordsworth, Keats, Shelley, Tennyson, Browning.

TEN GREATEST ENGLISH ESSAYISTS

Bacon, Addison, Steele, Macaulay, Lamb, Jeffrey, De Quincey, Carlyle, Thackeray and Matthew Arnold.

BEST PLAYS OF SHAKESPEARE

In order of merit are: *Hamlet, King Lear, Othello, Antony and Cleopatra, Macbeth, Merchant of Venice, Henry IV, As You Like It, Winter's Tale, Romeo and Juliet, Midsummer Night's Dream, Twelfth Night, Tempest.*

ONLY THE GOOD

If you are not able to procure a library of the great masterpieces, get at least a few. Read them carefully, intelligently and with a view to enlarging your own literary horizon. Remember a good book cannot be read too often, one of a deteriorating influence should not be read at all. In literature, as in all things else, the good alone should prevail.

```
Poster's  Note:  the  words  "encyclopoedia",  "insiduously",  and
"Synechdoche"
are thus in the original printing as are the spaces between "B. A."
etc.
"Insiduously" and "Synechdoche" are valid variant spellings.
```

The End

BN Publishing

www.bnpublishing.com

We have Book Recommendations for you

Automatic Wealth: The Secrets of the Millionaire Mind--Including: Acres of Diamonds, As a Man Thinketh, I Dare you!, The Science of Getting Rich, The Way to Wealth, and Think and Grow Rich [UNABRIDGED]
by Napoleon Hill, et al (CD-ROM - February 23, 2005)

Think and Grow Rich [MP3 AUDIO] [UNABRIDGED]
by Napoleon Hill, Jason McCoy (Narrator) (Audio CD - January 30, 2006)

As a Man Thinketh [UNABRIDGED]
by James Allen, Jason McCoy (Narrator) (Audio CD - May 1, 2005)

Your Invisible Power: How to Attain Your Desires by Letting Your Subconscious Mind Work for You [MP3 AUDIO] [UNABRIDGED]
by Genevieve Behrend, Jason McCoy (Narrator) (Audio CD - February 9, 2006)

Thought Vibration or the Law of Attraction in the Thought World [MP3 AUDIO] [UNABRIDGED]
by William Walker Atkinson, Jason McCoy (Narrator) (Audio CD - July 1, 2005)

Automatic Wealth, The Secrets of the Millionaire Mind-Including:As a Man Thinketh, The Science of Getting Rich, The Way to Wealth and Think and Grow Rich (Paperback)

www.bnpublishing.com